Eliza Ruhamah Scidmore

and Japan

The Life and Journeys to the Far East of

The American Woman Who Brought

"Sakura" to Washington, D.C.

Mayumi Itoh

For the souls of *sakura*,

and for those of who dedicated themselves

to bringing the cherry blossoms to Washington, D.C.

Contents

Note for paperback edition: This book is for on-demand printing. The actual page numbers (and page breaks and other formatting matters) may differ from the page numbers shown in the Table of Contents above, due to the formatting by Amazon that is used on the day of the book order.

List of Photographs

1. Eliza Ruhamah Scidmore, undated.

2. George Hawthorne Scidmore, undated.

3. Cover design of *Jinrikisha Days in Japan*, New York: Harper & Brother, 1891.

4. Japanese women picking tea leaves, undated.

5. Japanese farmers with their packhorse, undated.

6. Cherry blossom viewing at Ueno Park, 1897.

7. Cherry blossom viewing at Sumida River Bank at Mukōjima, 1897.

8. Helen Herron Taft (June 1861–May 1943), undated.

9. Helen Herron Taft Manning (August 1891–February 1987), only daughter of William H. Taft and Helen H. Taft, Yokohama, 1900.

10. David Fairchild, undated.

11. Takamine Jōkichi, undated.

12. Ozaki Yukio and Ozaki Yei Theodora, undated.

13. Burning of diseased Japanese cherry tree saplings, January 28, 1910.

14. New main building of Yokohama Nursery Company, built in 1905.

15. Meiji Sanriku Earthquake, June 1896.

16. Cover design of *As The Hague Ordains: Journal of a Russian Prisoner's Wife in Japan*, New York: Henry Holt, 1907.

17. Russian POW on a stretcher smoking a cigarette given by a Japanese soldier, Dalian, 1904.

18. Russian POWs in front of a theater in Matsuyama, 1904.

19. Russian POWs relaxing at a Japanese inn in Dōgo Onsen, 1904.

20. Graves for Russian POWs in Matsuyama, created in 1905.

21. Members of Glee Club organized by Russian POWs (sitting, the Japanese archbishop of the Nagoya Russian Orthodox Church), Nagoya, 1904.

22. Portrait of Nitobe Inazō on ¥5,000 bill.

23. Cover design of Inazo Nitobe's *Bushido: The Soul of Japan*, Philadelphia, PA: Leeds & Biddle, 1900.

24. Grave of the Scidmore family at the Yokohama Foreign General Cemetery.

25. Memorial stone for Eliza Ruhamah Scidmore at the

Yokohama Foreign General Cemetery, erected November 1929.

All translations were made by the author in the form of paraphrases, not as literal translations, in order for the translations to make sense in English without losing the original meaning. In so doing, evident mistakes and typos were corrected and some explanations were added, in order to facilitate an accurate understanding of the original text.

For spelling in Japanese, the Hepburn Romanization system is primarily used, with macrons; however, macrons are not used for words known in English without macrons, as for Kyoto and Tokyo. Another exception is that "n" is not converted to "m" for words where it precedes "b, m, and n"; for example, Saionji "Kinmochi," instead of Kimmochi. Names for Japanese newspapers, such as *Asahi Shimbun*, are given 'as is' because they are their official English names. In addition, some of the literature quoted in this book was written before the standard Romanization style was established, and used old spellings, such as "Kioto" (Kyoto) and "Tokio" (Tokyo). They are shown 'as is' in direct quotations.

Names of Japanese persons are given with the surname first, except for those who use the reversed order in English. Honorific prefixes, such as doctor and mister, are not used in the text, except in direct quotations. Positions and titles for individuals are as of the time for which the event is described in the particular passage of the text, unless specified otherwise. There was discrepant information on the dates of events. When the exact date could not be determined, this book provides two dates, as in 1906/1907, which means either 1906 or 1907.

Citation numbers for sources of information are normally given at the end of each paragraph, instead of at the end of each sentence, in order to enhance the smooth reading of the text, and also to limit the number of citations. Regarding online sources, the dates of actual access are given, unless the sources give the posting dates.

Acknowledgments

I would like to thank Tsuneo Akaha, Kent Calder, Toshiko Calder, Steve Clemons, Akiko Collcutt, Gerald Curtis, Joshua Fogel, Ronald Hrebenar, Ken Kawata, Donald Keene, Ellis Krauss, Mike Mochizuki, T. J. Pempel, Stephen Roddy, Gilbert Rozman, Richard Samuels, Vicki Wong, Donald Zagoria, and Quansheng Zhao, for continuous encouragement and inspirations. I extend my deep appreciation to Gregory Rewoldt and Megumi Itoh, for generous support.

—November 3, 2017

On the 89th memorial anniversary

of Eliza Ruhamah Scidmore's death

Abbreviations

DAR	Daughters of the American Revolution Hospital Corps
ICRC	International Committee of the Red Cross
IJA	Imperial Japanese Army
IPR	Institute of Pacific Relations
JR	Japan Railways
JRCS	Japanese Red Cross Society
MOFA	Ministry of Foreign Affairs
NYK	Nippon Yūsen Kaisha
POWs	Prisoners of War
UNESCO	United Nations Educational, Scientific and Cultural Organization

Map of Japan as related to Eliza Ruhamah Scidmore

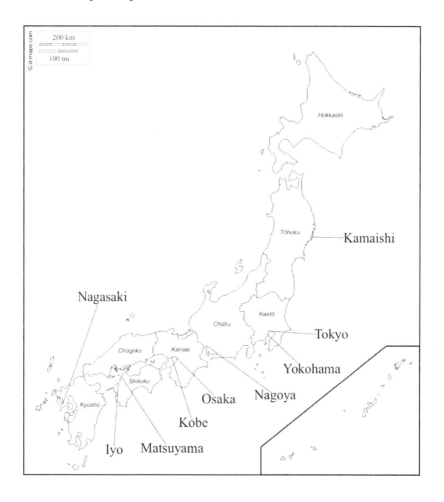

Source: Constructed by author from blank map of Japan, courtesy of Daniel Dalet, d-maps.com, http://d-maps.com/m/asia/japan/japonryukyu/japonryukyu42.gif

Photograph 1: Eliza Ruhamah Scidmore, undated. *Source*: "Eliza
Scidmore," undated, https://www.nps.gov/articles/eliza-
scidmore.htm, accessed July 16, 2017.

1. Introduction

On March 27, 2017, the National Cherry Blossom Festival was held in Washington, D.C., and as many as 1.5 million people visited the capital city in order to admire the cherry blossoms in West Potomac Park around the Tidal Basin. Today, it is almost forgotten that the spectacular view of cherry blossoms is owed to an inspiration of an American woman. Her name was Eliza Ruhamah Scidmore (pronounced "Sid-more," October 1856– November 1928). While visiting Japan in the mid-1880s, Scidmore was captivated by the beauty of the cherry blossoms in Tokyo and conceived the idea to transplant Japanese flowering cherry trees to the U.S. capital.[1]

Her idea finally materialized in 1912, when 3,020 saplings of Japanese flowering cherry trees arrived safely in Washington, D.C., as a gift of friendship to the people of the United States from the people of Japan, by the City of Tokyo (current Tokyo prefecture). The cherry tree saplings were successfully transplanted to the area around the Potomac Tidal Basin and to the Capitol grounds, on March 27, 1912 and afterwards. Twenty-three years later, on March 27, 1935, the first national cherry blossom festival was held in commemoration of the landmark event. This is the origin of the National Cherry Blossom Festival that has been celebrated annually, to this day.[2]

Scope of This Book

Eliza Ruhamah Scidmore was a pioneering female journalist/photographer. She explored the American frontiers, such as the Dakota territory and the Alaskan wilderness— including the Aleutians—and traveled extensively around the world. She wrote prolifically about her journeys in leading magazines such as *National Geographic* and *The Century Magazine*. She then successfully turned her travelogues into books—*Alaska, Its Southern Coast and the Sitkan Archipelago* (1885); *Westward to the Far East: A Guide to the Principal Cities of China and Japan* (1891); *Jinrikisha Days in Japan* (1891); *Appleton's Guide-Book to Alaska and the Northwest Coast: Including the Shores of Washington, British Columbia, Southeastern Alaska, the Aleutians and Seal Islands, the Bering and the Arctic Coasts* (1893); *Java, the Garden of the East* (1897); *China, the Long-Lived Empire* (1900); *Winter India* (1903); and *As The Hague Ordains: Journal of a Russian Prisoner's Wife in Japan* (1907).[3]

Scidmore neither wrote a memoir of her own nor left a record of her life. She was an observer of landscapes and people in them, never a protagonist of her stories. Although her writings still give a glimpse, many aspects of her personal life are still shrouded in mystery. To cover all of Scidmore's journeys would be beyond the scope of this book. This book instead focusses on her journeys to Japan and her association with Japan, because it was her visits to Japan that made her a proponent for the project of transplanting Japanese flowering cherry trees to Washington, D.C. In so doing, this book examines two compelling and memorable books she wrote about Japan: *Jinrikisha Days in Japan* (1891) and *As The Hague Ordains: Journal of a Russian Prisoner's Wife in Japan* (1907).

Part I   Early Years

*

2. Formative Years

Eliza Ruhamah Scidmore was born in Clinton, Iowa, on October 14, 1856, as the second child of George Bolles Scidmore and Eliza Catherine Scidmore. Soon after her birth, her family moved to Madison, Wisconsin, and she grew up there. Then, during the Civil War, her parents were separated and her mother moved to Washington, D.C., with her two children. Scidmore's mother was an enterprising and entertaining person and ran a boarding house, where Scidmore as a child met many politicians and visitors to the U.S. capital. She watched army troops marching through the streets and played on the White House grounds, where she often met and spoke to President Abraham Lincoln.[4]

In 1864, when she was eight years old and her elder brother was ten, her mother gave them each an autograph album. Then, the siblings went to the White House with their new autograph albums. President Lincoln took one of them on each knee, and wrote his name and theirs in them. In the boy's book, the president wrote, "For Master George H. Scidmore, A. Lincoln, Oct. 24, 1864." With this auspicious start, the siblings went the rounds of official and diplomatic circles and gathered an impressive

collection of autographs, including those of Andrew Johnson,

Ulysses S. Grant, and Rutherford B. Hayes. The autograph album

of George Scidmore is preserved in the Newberry Library in

Chicago, whereas Eliza's has been lost.[5]

As a teenager, Eliza Scidmore frequently attended social

functions and parties in the capital, and associated with influential

members of society. She also travelled to Europe and visited

England, Ireland, and Italy. Thus, in her formative years,

Scidmore nourished a keen interest in exotic places and foreign

cultures. Her interests were expansive, ranging from geography

and landscapes, to plants and flowers, and to fine arts and folk arts.[6]

3. Attending Oberlin College

Then, starting in 1873, Scidmore attended Oberlin College, in

Oberlin, Ohio. Founded in 1833, Oberlin College is one of the

most prestigious liberal arts colleges in the United States and is the

oldest coeducational liberal arts college in the country. In 1835,

the school also became the first college in the United States to

admit students of all races. In addition, its Conservatory of Music,

founded in 1865, is the oldest continuously operating conservatory

in the country. Its graduates include such luminaries as Jacob

Dolson Cox (October 1828–August 1900), Union Army general

and U.S. Secretary of the Interior in the Grant administration, and

Edwin O. Reischauer (October 1910–September 1990), Harvard-

Yenching Institute director and U.S. ambassador to Japan, as well

as Industrial Bank of Japan president Ono Eijirō (July 1864–

November 1927), the grandfather of Yoko Ono. The legendary

violin instructor at the Julliard School, Dorothy DeLay (March

1919–March 2004), attended the Oberlin Conservatory of Music

for one year. Also, Ōbirin (its phonetic rendition in Japanese)

University in Tokyo was named after Oberlin College, because its founder Shimizu Yasuzō (June 1891–January 1988) was a graduate of Oberlin College.[7]

At age 19, following two years of education at Oberlin College, Scidmore landed a job as a newspaper reporter, writing columns on social events in the U.S. capital for *The New York Times*, *St. Louis Globe-Democrat*, and *The Washington Post*. In 1876, she reported on the centennial celebration of the nation's independence, in Philadelphia. While covering the capital's social scene for several years, she grew more interested in exploring the frontiers of the United States and headed west to the Dakota Territory. Then, in 1883, she bought a ticket to Alaska, which the United States had purchased from Russia in March 1867. This was three decades before Alaska became a U.S. government territory in May 1912, and almost eight decades before Alaska was admitted as the 49th state in January 1959.[8]

4. Trips to Alaska

In the summer of 1883, Scidmore sailed through Alaska's Inside Passage (in southeastern Alaska) aboard the S.S. Idaho, with Captain James Carroll. They stopped at Glacier Bay to the north, marking the first time that tourists sailed into Glacier Bay. There, they met the indigenous Tlingit families and Dick Willoughby, one of the first Caucasian settlers in Alaska. Scidmore wrote about her encounters there in magazines and newspapers, including the Tlingit families hunting in Glacier Bay and Captain Carroll navigating the S.S. Idaho to the face of a tidewater glacier. After visiting Glacier Bay again in the summer of 1884, she successfully turned her articles into her first book, *Alaska, Its Southern Coast and the Sitkan Archipelago*, which was published in 1885. This is the first travel guide to Alaska ever written.[9]

Scidmore also befriended the renowned naturalist and environmental philosopher John Muir (April 1838–December 1914), who had discovered in 1879 that the ice in Glacier Bay had retreated almost all the way up the bay. Describing the Muir Glacier in Glacier Bay National Park and Reserve, named after

John Muir, Scidmore wrote: "Words and dry figures can give one little idea of the grandeur of this glacial torrent flowing steadily and solidly into the sea, and the beauty of the fantastic ice front, shimmering with all the prismatic hues, beyond imagery or description."[10]

Scidmore became one of the first Western women to travel to Glacier Bay and was instrumental in opening Alaska to mass tourism and ushering in the age of the Alaska cruise. For this contribution, a glacier is named after her at the location where she fell off from a horse and broke her collarbone. The Scidmore Glacier is nestled on the side of the Fairweather Mountains in Glacier Bay National Park. One cannot help but wonder what Scidmore would have felt had she learned of the rapidly shrinking glaciers in Alaska and elsewhere today, as well as of the fact that U.S. president Donald Trump announced in June 2017 that the U.S. government would withdraw from the Paris Climate Agreement, which stipulated international rules to combat the climate change and the global warming.[11]

Thus, Scidmore established her reputation as a pioneering female traveler and writer at a time when social norms kept women at home. Then, in 1884, her horizon expanded even further, when she traveled to the Far East to visit her elder brother, George Hawthorne Scidmore.

5. George Hawthorne Scidmore

George Hawthorne Scidmore (October 1854–November 1922) was born in Dubuque, Iowa in October 1854. Soon, the family moved to Clinton, Iowa, where Eliza was born, and then moved to Madison, Wisconsin. Then, during the Civil War, George, Eliza, and their mother moved to Washington, D.C. In 1876, George received a LL.B. degree from the Law Department of the National University (current George Washington University School of Law), was admitted to the bar of the District of Columbia, and began his diplomatic career in the same year. Because of his legal expertise, he is best known for his legal counselling, specifically in relation to extraterritorial functions in Japan.[12]

His first assignments took place in Europe: consular clerk at the U.S. Consulate General in Liverpool, England (1876–1877); secretary (or vice consul, depending on the source) in Dunfermline, Scotland (1877–1878); and secretary in Paris, France (1878–1880). Then, came assignments to the Far East: consular clerk at the U.S. Consulate General in Yokohama, Japan (1881–1884); vice consul in Osaka and Hyōgo (current Kobe, 1884–

1885); vice consul general in Shanghai, China (1885) during the Sino-French War; vice and deputy consul general in Kanagawa (part of current Yokohama, 1885–1891). He also served as commodore of the Yokohama Yacht Club for eight terms and, in March 1891, he was decorated by the Japanese emperor Mutsuhito for saving a Japanese from drowning.[13]

In 1891, George Scidmore was assigned to Fiji Islands (current Republic of Fiji) in Oceania—the British colony established in 1874—as special envoy of the U.S. State Department to investigate the claims of American citizens that their lands on the islands had been confiscated by the British government. He also acted as a barrister and solicitor before the British Consular Court. Subsequently, he was again assigned to the Far East: deputy consul general in Kanagawa (1894–1902); deputy consul general in Yokohama (1902–1904) until the outbreak of the Russo-Japanese War, when he was detailed to the U.S. Legation in Tokyo as legal adviser (1904–1907). Then he was appointed as consul in Nagasaki (1907–1909); consul in Kobe (1909); consul general in Seoul, Korea (1909–1913); and then consul general in Yokohama (1913–1922).[14]

Photograph 2: George Hawthorne Scidmore, undated. *Source*:

American Consular Bulletin, Vol. 3, No. 1, March 1921, 175,

http://www.afsa.org/sites/default/files/fsj-1921-03-march_0.pdf.

Meanwhile, George Scidmore was actively engaged in academic, cultural, and social exchanges, as a member of numerous organizations including the Asiatic Society of Japan and the American Asiatic Association (secretary for seven terms), and a 32nd degree Mason. He also taught American and English law, as a lecturer, at the Tokyo English Law College (current Chuo University) for several years. He wrote two books, one being entitled, *Outline Lectures on the History, Organization, Jurisdiction, and Practice of the Ministerial and Consular Courts of the Unites States of America in Japan* (1887), as well as numerous reports on international legal matters for the U.S. Department of State. During his service in Yokohama, he had sent for his mother and had her live with him there. She died in October 1916, at age 92. He was unmarried and devoted himself to diplomatic service, which ended in November 1922 with his death at age 68. He died at his home in Yokohama, where he was the incumbent U.S. consul general. In accordance with his will, his remains were cremated and buried with his mother in the Yokohama Foreign General Cemetery.[15]

6. Becoming a Correspondent for *National Geographic*

Eliza Scidmore, who also remained unmarried throughout her life, visited her brother on his diplomatic assignments. She therefore had the privilege to journey to many foreign countries, such as China, India, Japan, Java (then, a Dutch colony, part of current Indonesia), Korea, Russia, and possibly the Philippines (depending on the source). She visited many locales there that were inaccessible to ordinary travelers at that time. Meanwhile, in 1890, she joined the National Geographic Society, two years after its founding in 1888, and became a regular correspondent for *National Geographic* in 1893. There, she befriended National Geographic Society president Alexander Graham Bell, the inventor of telephone, and his family. Thus, she launched her prolific writing career in association with *National Geographic* and was appointed as the first female member of the Board of Trustees of the National Geographic Society. She continued to write for *National Geographic* for two decades until 1914.[16]

Part II   Scidmore Goes to Japan

7. Voyage to Japan

It is not established exactly when Scidmore visited Japan for the first time. Most of the Japanese researchers on Scidmore consider that she went to Japan for the first time in 1884. For instance, Tonosaki Katsuhisa, a member of the Project Promotion Committee of the Japan Cherry Blossom Society in Tokyo, who expertly translated Scidmore's *Jinrikisha Days in Japan* (1891), thinks that Scidmore arrived at Yokohama for the first time on September 11, 1884, when she was one month shy of 28 years old, via Shanghai, aboard the S.S. Tokyo-maru of Mitsubishi Trading Company. However, a few American sources, such as the National Park Service in Washington, D.C., state that Scidmore went to Japan for the first time in 1885.[17]

When Scidmore visited Japan, the nation was in the mid-Meiji period (January 1868–July 1912), with Emperor Mutsuhito (November 1852–July 1912) as the head of state, whose reign name was Meiji. With a highly centralized government modelled after the Bismarckian government of Germany, the Meiji government strove to transform Japan into a modern nation from the feudalistic society ruled by the Tokugawa shogunate government. Consequently, Japan was rapidly changing through its own Industrial Revolution, with slogans such as "Rich Nation, Strong Army" and "Enlightenment in Civilization."[18]

This visit sparked in Scidmore a profound interest in this exotic country in the Far East and an enduring association with its people, which lasted her lifetime. Scidmore visited Japan several times afterward (her name is on a passenger list from Yokohama to Seattle in July 1923). Her brother and mother moved around the Bund—the main avenue by the waterfront of Yokohama port— including addresses at the Club Hotel at 5 Bund, at 38 Bund, at 3 Bund, at 38B Bund, and finally at 6 Bund. Scidmore used the residence of her brother and mother in Yokohama as a base for her travels to local regions of Japan, as well as to other countries in the Far East, such as China, Korea, and as far as India and Java. (Today, the majestic Yokoyama Marine Tower stands on the main avenue overlooking the harbor.)[19]

Japan presented surprise after surprise to the American visitor, as Scidmore wrote, "All the Orient is a surprise to the

Occidental. Everything is strange with a certain unreality that makes one doubt half his sensations." Curiously, it was not the aspects of modernization and westernization of Japan that impressed Scidmore. Rather, she was fascinated by rural landscapes and the traditional way of living of the Japanese. From the moment she landed at Yokohama port, she fell under the spell of Japan, and wrote, "Japan is a dream of Paradise, beautiful from the first green island off the coast to the last picturesque hill-top...The bold and irregular coast is rich in color, the perennial green of the hill-side is deep and soft, and the perfect cone of Fujiyama against the sky completes the landscape[.]"[20]

8. Traveling Through Japan on a Rickshaw

Scidmore travelled all over Japan, riding on a *jinrikisha* (a two-wheeled rickshaw carriage pulled by one man). She marveled at its landscapes and intently observed the local folk culture. Among many strange scenes in the countryside, Scidmore took notice of the beauty and practicality of "rooftop gardening." Villagers grew flowers, such as irises and lilies, on top of the thatched roofs of traditional hut-like houses. The flowers not only provided a lovely view, but also strengthened the structure of the roof (lily bulbs were drought resistant and also served as food reserve for famines which happened often in olden days in Japan). Travelling through Yokohama, from Tokyo to Kamakura southward, she wrote, "All this part of Japan is old, and rich in temples, shrines, and picturesque villages, with a net-work of narrow roads and shady by-paths leading through perpetual scenes of beauty. Thatched roofs, whose ridge poles are beds of lilies, shaded by glorified green plumes of bamboo-trees, tall, red barked cryptomerias, crooked pines, and gnarled camphor-trees, everywhere charm the eye."[21]

Photograph 3: Cover design of Eliza Ruhamah Scidmore's

Jinrikisha Days in Japan, New York: Harper & Brothers, 1891.

Scidmore was also fascinated by Japanese landscape

gardens, which were aesthetically designed to recreate natural

landscapes. To the American traveler, these gardens must have

looked like miniature box gardens (*hakoniwa*) or "toy-gardens"

(*bonsai*). Noting the passion for flowers and gardens of the

Japanese, she referred to them as "necromancers" of plants. In turn, from the standards of the American way of living, the Japanese houses must have looked like doll houses, decorated with miniature furniture. In fact, Scidmore wrote that the "houses seem toys, their inhabitants dolls, whose manner of life is clean, pretty, artistic, and distinctive."[22]

Scidmore's observations evoke images of the island country of Lilliput in *Gulliver's Travels* (1726) by Jonathan Swift and *The Borrowers* (1952) by Mary Norton, of which an anime film version was made by the Tokyo-based Studio Ghibli in 2010, with the title "Arrietty, the Borrower" (or "The Secret World of Arrietty" in the North American release). Scidmore wrote of the Japanese way of life, "Every-day life looks too theatrical, too full of artistic and decorative effects, to be actual and serious, and streets and shops seem set with deliberately studied scenes and carefully posed groups." Scidmore also described the characteristics of the Japanese "as the fine flower of the Orient, the most polite, refined, and aesthetic of races, happy, light-hearted, friendly, and attractive."[23]

Photograph 4: Japanese women picking tea leaves, undated.

Source: Eliza Ruhamah Scidmore, *Jinrikisha Days in Japan*, New York: Harper & Brothers, 1891, 305.

As Scidmore travelled throughout Japan, she eagerly observed the daily life of the ordinary Japanese, as well as that of the high-class society, with her penetrating vision. She was fascinated by their sophisticated culture, in which townsfolk wrote poems as they watched flowers and the moon, and enjoyed cherry blossom tea and a salad made of chrysanthemum petals. She was also impressed with industrious farmers and enthralled by their traditions, in which they made almost everything they needed from bamboos and straws—they were not only practical but beautiful—and even made soft and warm straw-shoes for their horses. Their fine arts and folk arts were a marvelous fusion with nature. She compiled her vivid portrayals of the Japanese people and their lifestyle into *Jinrikisha Days in Japan* (1891), with scores of illustrations and several photographs.[24]

Photograph 5: Japanese farmers with their packhorse, undated.

Source: Eliza Ruhamah Scidmore, *Jinrikisha Days in Japan*, New York: Harper & Brothers, 1891, 163.

This book became a must-read for Americans who were interested in Japan or were planning to visit Japan. The significance of this book is that it is not only a fine travel guide, but also a first-class introduction to Japan. Her descriptions of Japanese culture, history, mores, and traditions are precise, which underscore her profound understanding of this exotic civilization. Her book became a classic for Japan study and she became an expert on Japan.[25]

9. Climbing Mt. Fuji

Being an intrepid explorer, Scidmore even climbed Mt. Fuji, or Fujiyama, a symbol of Japan, of which she wrote: "In summer Fuji's purple cone shows only ribbon stripes of white near its apex. For the rest of the year it is a slivery, shining vision, rivaled only by Mt. Rainier, which, pale with eternal snows, rises from the dense forests of Puget Sound to glass itself in those green waters."[26]

This description resonates with the experience of this author during the flight from Los Angeles to Seattle in June 1982, at a time when she had never heard of Scidmore, let alone had read her books. The pilot volunteered to act as a tour guide for the passengers, telling them to look left out the windows, and then right, and left again. The view of the mountains, such as the Cascade Range, was breathtaking. Even the pilot, who must have taken the same route many times, appeared to be impressed. The grand finale was Mt. Rainier, which looked like a giant Mt. Fuji. Coming from a small country, this author was awestruck with the grandeur of the majestic 'American Fujiyama.'

Scidmore chronicles her ascent of Fujiyama. In late July, a Western group of seven—four stalwart men and three valiant women including Scidmore—accompanied by two Japanese boys, or valets, headed to Miyanoshita, the famous summer resort at the foot of Fujiyama. There, they hired 15 guides/baggage coolies— nine of whom carried three *kago* (portable palanquins) for the three ladies until they reached Umagaeshi (*lit.*, "turn back horse"), at about a third of the height of the mountain, from which point no horses or palanquins were allowed, and the three ladies walked. Thus, the most unusual company of 24 people climbed the lava-trail laboriously. Fujiyama is one of the most sacred mountains of Shintoism in Japan, and the company on their way saw trains of descending pilgrims in white kimonos, who in turn were surprised to see the blue-eyed mountaineers and cheerfully greeted them.[27]

On the second day, the company was hit by a storm. They cautiously trailed on the lava-track, grabbing onto a rope, in the blinding rain and driving wind, until they arrived at a shelter, a mountain hut, at Number Eight (the eighth height point of the mountain). Then, the whirling storm kept them trapped in the log cabin for three nights. Yet, on the third day, taking advantage of a gap in the clouds, they hurriedly ascended to the summit. However, no sooner had they received certificates of ascent to the summit from a shrine priest than they were forced to leave the summit, as the wind rose and the whirling rain came on. Thus, undaunted by the brutal storms and having been trapped in the mountain hut for three days, the company achieved its goal, and Scidmore became one of the first Western women to reach the top of Mt. Fuji.[28]

10. Captivated by Cherry Blossoms

Among the many things that captivated Scidmore in Japan was the cherry blossoms or "*sakura*," which she called "the most beautiful thing in the world." If Fujiyama is the majestic symbol of Japan, the *sakura* is the fragile symbol of Japan. She wrote: "Even more beautiful than the plum-tree festival is the Tokio [Tokyo] celebration of the blossoming of the cherry, and gayer than the brilliant throngs are the marvelous trees...A faint fragrance arises from these sheets of bloom, but the strange glare of pinkish light from their fair canopy dazzles and dizzies the beholder."[29]

However, it was not only the aesthetic beauty of the cherry blossoms that impressed Scidmore. She was also fascinated by the way the Japanese admired and appreciated the cherry blossoms. Cherry blossoms are the favorite flowers among the Japanese so that *hana* (*lit.*, flower) refers to a cherry blossom in art and literature, although the cherry blossom has its own name, *sakura*. Similarly, *hana-mi* (flower viewing) refers to cherry blossom viewing, not just any flower viewing. Scidmore observed that when the cherry blossom season came, the passion for flowers of the Japanese reached its peak. Scidmore even doubted her own eyes to find the Japanese, who were usually shy and serious, came outside and had picnics under the cherry trees, drinking sake in public and singing and dancing merrily. She was surprised to discover the social significance of *hana-mi* that functioned as an occasion for people to get together with their families and friends.[30]

Visiting popular cherry blossom viewing spots, such as Ueno Park and Mukōjima by the Sumida River in downtown Tokyo, Scidmore wrote: "Not the Bois, the Cascine, or the Thier Garten can vie with Uyéno on this blossom Sunday...The cherry-blossom Sunday of Uyéno Park is a holiday of the upper middle class. One week later, the double avenue of blossoming trees, lining the Mukojima for a mile along the river bank, invites the lower classes to a very different celebration from that of the decorous, well-dressed throng driving, walking, picnicking, and tea drinking under the famous trees."[31]

Photograph 6: Cherry blossom viewing at Ueno Park, 1897.

Source: "The Hanamai (Flower-Picnic),"

http://www.baxleystamps.com/litho/ogawa/ogawa_hanami.shtml,

from Takashima Suteta, *The Hanamai* (*Flower Picnic*), Tokyo:

Ogawa Kazumasa Photo Studio, 1897.

Scidmore adds:

Czars and Kaisers may well envy this Oriental ruler, whose

subjects gather by thousands, not to throw bombs and riot

for bread or the division of property, but to fall in love with cherry-trees, and write poems in their praise. Mukojima's carnival rivals the saturnalia of the ancients...Men dance like satyrs, cup and gourd [of sake] in hand, or extending a hand, make orations to the crowd—natural actors, orators, and pantomimists every one of them. But with all this intoxication, only glee and affection manifest themselves. No fighting, no rowdyism, no rough words accompany the spring saturnalia; and the laughter is so infections, the antics and figures so comical, that even sober people seem to have tasted of the insane cup.[32]

Photograph 7: Cherry blossom viewing at Sumida River Bank at

Mukōjima, 1897. *Source*: "The Hanamai (Flower-Picnic),"

http://www.baxleystamps.com/litho/ogawa/ogawa_hanami.shtml,

from Takashima Suteta, *The Hanamai* (*Flower Picnic*), Tokyo:

Ogawa Kazumasa Photo Studio, 1897.

In 1918, the future Chinese premier Zhou Enlai (March

1898–January 1976), who was studying in Tokyo, also went out to

see the cherry blossoms in Ueno Park and Mukōjima. Just as

Scidmore was, the young Zhou was captivated by the fragile beauty of the *sakura*. On his way home in early April 1919, he visited Kyoto and saw the cherry blossoms there. He was enthralled by their beauty so that he visited Arashiyama Park twice and Maruyama Park four times, and wrote four poems about the *sakura* in Kyoto. Undoubtedly, Scidmore herself visited Arashiyama Park and Maruyama Park, admired their *sakuras*, and wrote about them.[33]

Scidmore further discovered that cherry blossoms not only generated festivity among Japanese but also seeped into the Japanese culture and even into their spirituality. She realized that the cherry blossoms represented "the soul of Japan." The fragility of cherry blossoms symbolized the Japanese ethos of *mono no aware* (the sadness of all the things in the world) and their view of the ephemerality of life. Associating the transient nature of human life with that of *sakura*, the Japanese have kept writing poems about *sakura*, many of which were written as 'dying poems.' Later, in March 1910, Scidmore wrote in *The Century Magazine*:

> No other flower in all the world is so beloved, so exalted, so worshiped, as *sakura-no-hana*, the cherry-blossom of

53

Japan. It is not only the national flower, but the symbol of purity, the emblem of chivalry and knightly honor, the crest of a cult the vernal celebration of which has been observed with unflagging zeal for at least two thousand years.[34]

Part III   Scidmore and Japanese

Cherry Tree Transplanting Project

11. Becoming a Proponent for Transplanting Japanese Flowering Cherry Trees to Washington, D.C.

In the mid-1880s, Scidmore told herself, "What a marvelous culture! I wish I could make a place like Mukōjima in my homeland. I wish I could make the capital of my country full of cherry blossoms. The beautiful cherry trees that bloom every year will make the friendship between Americans and Japanese forever." Thus, was born Scidmore's vision of Japanese cherry blossoms around the Potomac Tidal Basin. Back in Washington, D.C., she became a proponent of a project to transplant Japanese flowering cherry trees to the U.S. capital. She first wrote to the superintendent of the U.S. Office of Public Buildings and Grounds and proposed that Japanese flowering cherry trees be planted along the reclaimed Potomac waterfront. However, being reluctant to import cherry trees from Asia, the superintendent told Scidmore: "It is dangerous to plant cherry trees around the waterfront, because children might climb the trees to pick cherries and fall in the river." Scidmore said: "The species of the cherry trees that I am proposing do not bear the fruits of cherries." Then, the superintendent said: "There is no point in planting such useless trees."[35]

Most of Americans at that time were not interested in the species of cherry trees that produced pretty blossoms because they did not bear the fruit of sweet cherries. Consequently, Scidmore's idea went into hiatus and she focused on writing travel guides of Alaska and the Far East. She also became an advocate for the new conservation movement for the creation of National Forest Reserves. In support of the newly passed Forest Reserve Act in 1891, Scidmore wrote a letter to the editor of *The Century Magazine*, which was published in September 1893. Meanwhile, Scidmore never gave up her idea about the Japanese cherry trees. She persisted and approached every new superintendent for two decades, but to no avail. Then, in 1904, when she learned of a plan to establish a park on the reclaimed land along the Potomac River, she grew even more determined to realize her idea.[36]

12. First Lady Helen Herron Taft

In 1909, Scidmore decided to raise the money to purchase the Japanese flowering cherry trees and sent a letter proposing her project to the new first lady. This was Helen Herron Taft (June 1861–May 1943), the first lady of 27th U.S. President William Howard Taft (September 1857–March 1930; term of office, March 1909–March 1913). Scidmore had already been acquainted with "Nellie" Taft, as her family referred to her, and was aware that the first lady knew about the cherry blossoms in Japan. William Taft had served as governor general of the U.S. civil government in the Philippines from 1900 to 1903, after the U.S. government had taken over the islands from Spain, and Helen Taft had moved with their children to Manila. Before assuming the post, the Tafts stopped over Japan and arrived at Yokohama on May 10, 1900. Thus, they missed the cherry blossoms by a month, but they were granted a special meeting with Emperor Mutsuhito and Empress Haruko. While William Taft soon headed to Manila, Helen Taft and their three children stayed in Yokohama for three months until August 10, 1900.[37]

Photograph 8: Helen Herron Taft (June 1861–May 1943),

undated. *Source*: Helen Herron Taft, *Recollections of Full Years*,

New York: Dudd, Mead, 1914, unnumbered front page.

Then, in early February 1904, just after William Taft was appointed as U.S. secretary of war at the outbreak of the Russo-Japanese War (February 1904– September 1905), the couple briefly stopped over in Japan again, and received exceptional hospitality, including a luncheon at the Imperial Palace. The couple also visited Tokyo in July 1905, when Taft, as U.S. special envoy, made the secret Taft–Katsura Memorandum with prime minister Katsura Tarō, in which they agreed, in the aftermath of Japan's victory in the Russo-Japanese War, that Japan would have control over Korea while the United States would have control over the Philippines. Japanese deputy foreign minister Chinda Sutemi, who would become ambassador to the United States in 1912 (examined below), acted as interpreter. The couple also visited Japan in the fall of 1906 (or 1907) during the first cabinet of Saionji Kinmochi (term of office, January 1906–July 1908), and lunched at the Shiba Detached Imperial Palace, and met with such heroes of the Russo-Japanese War as Marshal-Admiral Tōgō Heihachirō (who is dubbed the "Nelson of the East") and Field Marshal Ōyama Iwao.[38]

From these accounts of Helen Taft, it seems unlikely that she actually saw cherry blossoms in Japan. The only possible time that she could have seen cherry blossoms there was when the couple visited Japan in February 1904. Some of the species of early bloomers could bloom in February, but she did not mention them in her memoir. At least she must have seen paintings and other art objects depicting cherry blossoms, during her stay in Japan with her children and visits to Japan with her husband.

Photograph 9: Helen Herron Taft Manning (August 1891–
February 1987), only daughter of William H. Taft and Helen H.
Taft, in Yokohama, 1900. *Source*: Helen Herron Taft,
Recollections of Full Years, New York: Dudd, Mead, 1914, in
between pages 76 and 77.

Although Helen Taft might have missed the cherry blossoms during her brief sojourns in Japan, interestingly, she did meet Scidmore's mother and brother there. Eliza Catherine Scidmore entertained the Tafts in her house on the Bund in Yokohama, and befriended them. Helen Taft recalled, "[Mrs. Scidmore's] son was in the Legation service when I met her and she had a charming house on the Bund, in which was gathered a remarkable collection of Japanese curios and objects of art. Mrs. Scidmore was then nearly eighty year of age I think, but she was as bright and young as a woman of fifty. The last time I saw her she was nearly ninety and she entertained us at luncheon in Nagasaki, where her son was American Consul....She afterward went to 'keep house' for her son in Seoul, Korea, where he became Consul General, and she continued to be a sort of uncrowned queen of foreign society." She was a gracious host, "with great animation and entire comprehension, general topics of current interest."[39]

In turn, Helen Taft referred to Eliza Ruhamah Scidmore as "the well known writer about Far Eastern countries, and is, I suppose, the most notable foreign figure in the Orient." Scidmore might have inherited her mother's dispositions, as she was known at Dupont Circle to have a "superb physique…full of varying expression and humor." She was "a brilliant conversationalist with a keen, trenchant humor…possessed of an inexhaustible fund of anecdotes and reminiscence of interesting people."[40]

Then, upon the inauguration of President Taft in March 1909, the Helen Taft took charge of the project to beautify the reclaimed land along the Potomac River. She actually planned to "convert Potomac Park into a glorified Luneta where all Washington could meet, either on foot or in vehicles, at five o'clock on certain evenings, listen to band concerts and enjoy such recreation as no other spot in Washington could possibly afford." Luneta refers to Rizal Park in Manila, where the Tafts lived from 1900 to 1903.[41]

Two days after Scidmore had sent her letter to the first lady, Helen Taft responded and wrote a reply dated April 7, 1909:

> Thank you very much for your suggestion about the cherry trees. I have taken the matter up and am promised the trees, but I thought perhaps it would be best to make an avenue of them, extending down to the turn in the road, as

64

the other part is still too rough to do any planting. Of course, they could not reflect in the water, but the effect would be very lovely of the long avenue. Let me know what you think about this. Sincerely yours, Helen H. Taft[42]

Thus, Scidmore found a most powerful ally in the first lady and Scidmore's "time-worn plea" finally moved forward almost a quarter century after she had conceived the idea in the mid-1880s. In order to accomplish this, however, she still needed much help from American government officials, as well as from the Japanese government authorities concerned. Initially, the first lady tried to collect flowering cherry trees domestically, and the superintendent of the Office of Public Buildings and Grounds, Colonel Spencer Cosby, made the purchase of 90 Japanese cherry trees from a nursery in Pennsylvania and planted them along the Potomac. However, this did not work and all of the cherry trees apparently died soon.[43]

13. Botanist and Plant Prospector David Fairchild

In 1909, Eliza Scidmore lived in the fashionable Shoreham Hotel in the District of Columbia. From there, she relaunched her Japanese cherry tree project. For instance, in the letter addressed to David Fairchild dated April 27, 1909, which is preserved today, she asked for contact information for importing flowering cherry trees from Japan. David Fairchild (April 1869–August 1954) was a member of the respectable Fairchild family, descendants of Thomas Fairchild. David's great uncle, James Fairchild, was president of Oberlin College, while David's father, George Fairchild, was president of the Kansas State College of Agriculture (current Kansas State University), from which David graduated.[44]

Photograph 10: David Fairchild, undated. *Source*: "History of the Cherry Trees," undated, https://www.nps.gov/subjects/cherryblossom/history-of-the-cherry-trees.htm, accessed July 16, 2017.

David Fairchild became a distinguished botanist and plant explorer/prospector in his own right and was appointed as the first director of the Office of Seed and Plant Introduction of the U.S. Department of Agriculture at its inception in 1898. In 1905, Fairchild married Marian Bell, the younger daughter of Alexander Graham Bell. The famous inventor was also president of the National Geographic Society and Fairchild served as a member of its board of trustees. In 1928, he built a home in Coconut Grove, Florida, which is part of the National Tropical Botanical Garden today. In 1938, the Fairchild Tropical Botanic Garden was created in Coral Gables in Florida, named after him.[45]

Fairchild's association with Japanese flowering cherry trees began in December 1901, when he visited Japan for the first time during his prospecting tour of the world. He befriended Yokohama Nursery Company founding president Suzuki Uhei, who suggested that he secure a collection of Japanese flowering cherry trees, and showed him innumerable varieties in their autumn foliage. Fairchild was impressed with the meticulously cared-for plants and manicured bonsai pots at the nursery, and wrote in *The*

World Was My Garden: Travels of a Plant Explorer (1938) that

"The low, unpainted wooden buildings of the nursery were of

charming proportions and pleasing color. The packing sheds

presented a beautiful and animated scene…On the long pine tables

were neatly arranged creations of Japanese hor[t]icultural

art…Whenever I looked into the finder [of my camera], the image

made a charming picture. It seems incredible that a nursey could

be so completely picturesque."[46]

Then, a Japanese tree doctor showed Fairchild the drawing

of the Japanese flowering cherry trees, and he felt, "I have rarely

been so thrilled, for I had had no idea of the wealth of beauty,

form, and color of the flowering cherries." In 1938, he wrote, "I

was sorry, very sorry to leave Japan, and I have often wanted to go

back. But I hear that the rickshaws are gone, that motor roads have

been built everywhere, and the picturesque costumes of the men [at

the Yokohama Nursery Company] have disappeared. I could not

bear to see the workmen wearing ugly American straw hats. I

would rather keep my memories of old Japan as it was at the

beginning of the century." Scidmore, who had also visited the

Yokohama Nursery Company during her sojourns in Japan, could not have agreed more. Fairchild would be pleased to know that Yokohama Nursery Company employees today wear a modern version of their traditional uniform jackets with the company's logo.[47]

Back home in 1906, Fairchild imported 75 Japanese flowering cherry trees and 25 Japanese weeping cherry trees privately from the Yokohama Nursery Company. He planted them on his own estate in Chevy Chase, Maryland, in order to test their hardiness. His experiment worked and in 1907 he began to lobby for planting Japanese flowering cherry trees along the avenues in the District of Columbia. In 1908, Fairchild gave saplings of the cherry trees to children from each school in the District so that they could plant them in their schoolyard for the observance of Arbor Day (observed on the last Friday in April in the District of Columbia). He invited Scidmore, "then the most noted writer on Japan," to his Arbor Day lecture and appealed that the "Speedway" (which referred to parts of the avenues around the Potomac Tidal Basin, built for fast horse carriages) be transformed into "Fields of Sakura."[48]

In this context, Scidmore asked Fairchild for his advice on importing flowering cherry trees from Japan.

14. Biochemist and Philanthropist Takamine Jōkichi

No sooner had Scidmore's plan became public than the news reached Japanese communities on the East Coast and moved them. Among them, Takamine Jōkichi (December 1854–July 1922) became an avid supporter of Scidmore's project and was most instrumental in realizing it. Born as the son of the doctor for the lord of Kaga province in Kanazawa (in current Ishikawa prefecture), Takamine became a renowned biochemist and industrialist, who succeeded in isolating an enzyme that catalyzed the breakdown of starch. The enzyme was named 'takadiastase,' after his name. He worked in the Japanese Department of Agriculture and Commerce, which sent him to the 1884 World Fair, the World's Industrial and Cotton Centennial Exposition, held in New Orleans, as a co-commissioner. There, he met Caroline Hitch, his future wife, and also a newspaper reporter by the name of Lafcadio Hearn, who would be naturalized in Japan in 1896 (see Chapter 23).[49]

In 1890, after marrying Caroline Hitch, Takamine moved to the United States permanently—first residing in Chicago and then in New York City. Takamine made a fortune from his patent, "Process of Making Diastatic Enzyme," in 1894, the first patent for a microbial enzyme in the United States. Then, in 1900, he discovered and crystallized adrenalin, the first hormone to be isolated in the twentieth century. However, he went through more than a fair share of trials and tribulations in the United States. He was not allowed to become a U.S. citizen because the U.S. Naturalization Law at that time barred Japanese citizens from being naturalized. Asian immigrants were denied basic civil rights and there was widespread discrimination against Japanese. Worse, American malt manufacturers, who had resented the discovery of takadiastase, raided Takamine's home and tried to assassinate him (he escaped) and then burned down his research laboratory. He died in New York City in 1922, at age 67. His mausoleum stands in the respectable Woodlawn Cemetery in Bronx today.[50]

Takamine had an important mission of his own in supporting Scidmore's project. After the end of the Russo-Japanese War (February 1904– September 1905), American sentiment toward the Japanese diametrically changed, from a favorable to an unfavorable one. The American sentiment about the war was in favor of Japan because they had perceived Russia as a greater threat. To surprise within and without Japan, the small country that had just begun its modernization in 1868 defeated the huge empire. Japan owed its victory in part to the support of Americans, including that of Wall Street banker and philanthropist Jacob H. Schiff (January 1847–September 1920), who extended loans to Japan in the amount of $200 million (about $33 billion today). This was the first major flotation of Japanese bonds on Wall Street and provided about half the funds needed for Japan's war effort. Schiff's loans suggested a message against Tsarist Russia's anti-Semitic actions. Also, Russia was faced with serious internal unrest that led to the First Russian Revolution of June 1905.[51]

However, once the war ended, Americans began to perceive Japan as a threat. Japanese immigrants were industrious and worked hard on farmland on the West Coast. Especially in California, anti-Japanese sentiment ran high, as the residents who were themselves immigrants from other parts of the world felt that Japanese immigrants were taking away their jobs. Takamine wanted to alleviate the anti-Japanese sentiment by making a sincere gesture of Japanese friendship toward Americans, because he believed that grassroots exchanges would build up friendship and understanding between Americans and Japanese. Like a respectable samurai, Takamine diplomatically responded to anti-Japanese demonstrations on the West Coast that sought to segregate Japanese schoolchildren (specifically in San Francisco) and restrict Japanese immigration (see Chapter 31). In 1928, John H. Finley, president of City College of New York and commissioner of Education of the State of New York, wrote of Takamine:

> Born Samurai, a Far East Knight,
>
> He yielded his two swords to fight
>
> With science' weapons man's real foes—
>
> To lengthen life and stanch its woes.[52]

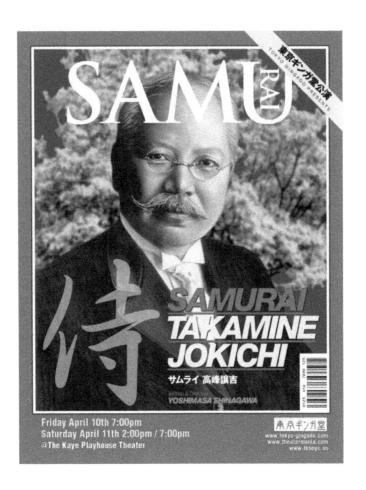

Photograph 11: Takamine Jōkichi, undated. *Source*: "The History of Enzyme Supplements," undated, http://deerlandenzymes.com/swallow/the-history-of-enzyme-supplements/, accessed July 23, 2017.

Against this backdrop, Takamine, an "unofficial ambassador," decided to donate his fortune to Scidmore's project.

Concurrently, Takamine, as president of the Japan Society of New York (of which Scidmore was a member), had been trying to beautify the Hudson River bank by planting Japanese cherry trees and in 1909 spent his fortune to transplant 2,000 Japanese cherry trees to Claremont Park (the location of current Sakura Park) near Grant's Tomb in Riverside Park in New York City, for the Hudson–Fulton Celebration. This was to commemorate the centennial of Robert Fulton's successful demonstration of the steam-powered boat on the Hudson River and the tercentenary of Henry Hudson's discovery of the Hudson River. However, the steamship that carried the tree saplings was lost en route to the United States. Undiscouraged, Takamine made a new donation of 3,000 Japanese cherry trees in 1912. Nevertheless, Takamine's name seldom appears in the official records of New York City park services, because he did not wish to receive credit for the donations and instead made the donations in the name of the City of Tokyo.[53]

On April 8, 1909, the day after first lady Nellie Taft wrote a reply to Scidmore, Takamine was in Washington, and so was the Japanese consul general in New York, Mizuno Kōkichi. Takamine, Mizuno, and Scidmore had known each other and the three got together. In the White House, they met Helen Taft and discussed Scidmore's plan. Mizuno suggested to the first lady that 2,000 Japanese flowering cherry trees be donated in the name of the City of Tokyo. She gladly accepted the proposal.[54]

15. Tokyo City Mayor Ozaki Yukio

Tokyo City Mayor Ozaki Yukio (December 1858–October 1954, commonly known by his penname, Ozaki Gakudō) was married to Yei (Eiko) Theodora, whose mother was English. Due to his liberal politics and his longest-serving time in the history of the Japanese national parliament, from its birth in 1890 to 1953, he is referred to as the "god of constitutional government" and the "founding father of parliamentary politics" in Japan. After the Russo-Japanese War, Ozaki was looking for a gracious gesture to reciprocate the favor that Japan had received from Americans during the war, such as the Wall Street banker Jacob H. Schiff.[55]

Photograph 12: Ozaki Yukio and Ozaki Yei Theodora, undated.

Source: "History of the Cherry Trees," undated,

https://www.nps.gov/subjects/cherryblossom/history-of-the-cherry-

trees.htm, accessed July 16, 2017.

Also, in August 1905, U.S. president Theodore Roosevelt

(October 1858–January 1919; term of office, September 1901–

March 1909) provided his good offices to end the war and hosted

25 delegates from Japan and Russia at the Hotel Wentworth in

New Castle, New Hampshire, for 30 days (the hotel

accommodated them at no charge). In September 1905, the delegates of the two countries signed a peace treaty at Portsmouth Naval Shipyard in Kittery, at the southern end of Maine: the Treaty of Portsmouth. In 1906, President Roosevelt received the Nobel Peace Prize for this role. Built in 1874, the historic landmark Hotel Wentworth is still in business as Wentworth by the Sea, A Marriott Hotel & Spa.[56]

Ozaki writes in his autobiography, "At the time of the war with Russia, the United States had shown enormous goodwill toward Japan. Jacob Schiff, a powerful American financier, was particularly helpful with regard to the issue of our foreign bonds. I had always wanted to express fitting appreciation for his kindness…but kept my thought to myself, because I thought the time was not right and expressing them prematurely might impede rather than advance the project…it was the government [of Japan] that should have offered gratitude to the U.S. for its kindness during the war, but there was no one in the Katsura government [of Army General Katsura Tarō] who thought of this. I knew that it might seem improper to have the suggestion come from the mayor of Tokyo, but nevertheless I was convinced that it was something that should be considered."[57]

With this background, Tokyo City Mayor Ozaki wanted to send a gift of appreciation to the White House. Thus, the Japanese Ministry of Foreign Affairs (MOFA) conveyed Mayor Ozaki's wish to Japanese consul general Mizuno, who in turn conveyed it to Takamine Jōkichi. Thus, began a collaboration between Mayor Ozaki in Tokyo and Takamine in New York City. Takamine went out of his way and donated his fortune to Scidmore's project. With the financial resources secured, the Japanese Embassy in Washington, D.C. officially informed the U.S. Department of State in August 1909 that 2,000 Japanese cherry trees would be donated by the City of Tokyo. Thus, it took almost a quarter century for Scidmore's vision to finally come true after she had conceived the idea.[58]

16.   First Shipment of 2,015 Japanese Flowering Cherry Trees

On behalf of Tokyo City Mayor Ozaki, Takamine had the Japanese MOFA collect 2,015 saplings of flowering cherry trees in Japan. Then, Nippon Yūsen Kaisha (NYK), the major Japanese shipping company, volunteered to ship the saplings free of charge. On November 24, 1909, NYK S.S. Kaga-maru left Yokohama port, bound for Seattle, carrying the saplings. On December 10, the S.S. Kaga-maru arrived in Seattle. Then, the shipment of saplings finally arrived in Washington, D.C on January 6, 1910. Nevertheless, no one had anticipated what would happen. It turned out that the plant quarantine inspection of the U.S. Department of Agriculture found that all of the Japanese cherry tree saplings were infested with insects and nematodes, and were seriously diseased. The inspection team concluded that all of the saplings had to be destroyed. On January 28, 1910, President William Taft granted his consent to burn them. Consequently, all of the 2,015 saplings were burned.[59]

Photograph 13: Burning of diseased Japanese cherry tree saplings, January 28, 1910. *Source*: "History of the Cherry Trees," undated, https://www.nps.gov/subjects/cherryblossom /history-of-the-cherry-trees.htm, accessed July 16, 2017.

The failure almost resulted a diplomatic issue between Japan and the United States. David Fairchild recalled in 1938, "I had been worried about the trees, fearing that they might prove too large, but I had not dreamed of any difficulty with the Quarantine authorities;...I found myself in a hornets' nest of protesting pathologists and entomologists, who were all demanding the destruction of the entire shipment." Worse, Fairchild wrote, Commander Richmond P. Hobson (U.S. Navy rear admiral and U.S. representative from Alabama) "chose just this moment to speak on the floor of Congress in a derogatory way of the Japanese. This, added to the disgust of Miss Scidmore, the annoyance of Major Cosby, the criticism of the pathologists and entomologists, and the astonishment of my Japanese friends, combined to give me many sleepless nights."[60]

Fairchild adds, "My only comfort was the knowledge that the trees had been so large, and their roots had been so cut, that I felt sure the greater number of them would have perished in the raw soil of the Speedway." Then, the "entire matter was finally hushed up." In later years, when Fairchild met Scidmore in Geneva, she told him "of a meeting in Mayor Osaki's [sic] office at which it was suggested that if the American public felt toward the Japanese as Commander Hobson's speech seemed to indicate, the matter of the flowering cherries had better be dropped." "Fortunately, more generous counsels prevailed" in 1910 in Washington, D.C.[61]

To the great relief of the U.S. officials concerned, Tokyo City mayor Ozaki Yukio responded to the burning of the cherry trees with humor. Quoting the anecdote about George Washington, Ozaki stated to the acting American ambassador in Tokyo, who looked somewhat troubled, "To be honest about it! It has been an American tradition to destroy cherry trees ever since your first president, George Washington!" Then, the acting ambassador withdrew, looking very relieved.[62]

Fujisaki Ichirō, Japanese ambassador to the United States (2008–2012), tells an inside story: The U.S. authorities were still concerned with the American sentiment that was not in favor of planting unfamiliar trees from Asia, infested with bugs, so that the U.S. Department of State issued a directive to the Japanese Embassy in Washington, D.C. It stated that specialists in both countries should study and work out a sound system for sending such trees to the United States, and that the Japanese side should refrain from attempting such a thing again until that time. It also gave warning to Takamine Jōkichi, who was concurrently trying to plant the Japanese flowering cherry trees in New York City.[63]

Japanese Plan for Second Donation

Scidmore was deeply disheartened by this and felt that it was an impossible idea to transplant cherry trees from 6,250 miles away, to begin with. Yet, this was not the end of the story. Contrary to the pessimism prevailed in Washington, D.C., Tokyo City Mayor Ozaki and Takamine were undeterred by the disaster. Ozaki writes, "If I did nothing further Americans would not learn of our goodwill, so I decided that cherry tree seeds should be planted in sterilized beds under the jurisdiction of the Ministry of Agriculture and Commerce. In this way we could nurse a new batch of cherry trees [free of pests and microbes]."[64]

Uchida 'Yasuya' (also pronounced Kōsai), the new Japanese ambassador to the United States and soon to be foreign minister (he served as foreign minister three times in three different cabinets), also felt that Japan should send another consignment, and as early as January 31, 1910, advised Tokyo that Japan would make a second donation. Then, on April 21, the Tokyo City Assembly authorized Mayor Ozaki's proposal. On behalf of Mayor Ozaki and Takamine, the Japanese MOFA collected new saplings of cherry trees. Remarkably, in two years from the disaster, the MOFA secured 3,020 new saplings of cherry trees, more than a 1,000 increase from the first donation. Fujisaki Ichirō wrote in 2012 that Ambassador Uchida was right because, had the Japanese not made the second shipment, history would have had it that Japan sent a weird gift to the United States, fueling the anti-Japanese sentiment in the country, and no such hallmark of friendship between Japan and the United States would have been made in Washington, D.C., which is enjoyed today.[65]

In 1910, the Japanese MOFA commissioned plant experts to make budwood (to be grafted onto the rootstock of another tree) out of the Somei-Yoshino—the most popular species of Japanese flowering cherry tree—that had grown by the Arakawa River in Adachi ward on the edge of Tokyo. This is close to Mukōjima where Scidmore had marveled at the cherry blossoms. In turn, the rootstock for the grafting was carefully selected from cherry trees in Itami, near Kobe in Hyōgo prefecture. For the purpose of diversity, to the 1,800 Somei-Yoshino, 11 other species of Japanese flowering cherry trees were added: 100 Ariake, 120 Fugenzo, 50 Fukurokuji, 20 Goyiko; 160 Ichiyo, 80 Jonioi, 350

Kwanzan (Kanzan), 20 Mikurumagaeshi, 130 Shirayuki, 50 Surugadainioi, and 140 Takinioi. Among them, all of the 20 Goyiko, whose name alludes to a "wish of an emperor," were designated to be planted on the White House Grounds, instead of by the Potomac Tidal Basin.[66]

The names of the species of Japanese flowering cherry trees gave American botanists, including David Fairchild, "a nomenclatorial tangle" and "chaotic confusion." For instance, Mikurumagaeshi, which is known for snowy blossoms, was given its literal translation, "Royal Carriage Turns Again to Look and See." Fairchild felt that it would be best to keep their original Japanese names intact.[67]

17. Second Shipment of 3,020 Japanese Flowering Cherry Trees

Before sending the second shipment of 3,020 saplings of Japanese flowering cherry trees, Tokyo City Mayor Ozaki wrote on February 2, 1912 to the U.S. Superintendent of Public Buildings and Parks stating, "Although a small token of the very high esteem in which the people of this city hold your great country, it gives them boundless pleasure to think that the trees may in a measure add to the embellishment of your magnificent capital. As for the first lot of trees which we sent you three years ago, we are more satisfied that you dealt with them as you did, for it would have pained us endlessly to have them retain a permanent source of trouble. The present trees have been raised under the special care of scientific experts and are reasonably expected to be free from the defects of their predecessors."[68]

The Japanese MOFA this time commissioned the Yokohama Nursery Company to pack and ship the 3,020 saplings of the Japanese flowering cherry trees. Founded in 1890, the Yokohama Nursery Company is a venerable institution, as David

Fairchild and Eliza Scidmore had visited there, and is still in business today. In 1912, the company packed the saplings and transported them to Yokohama port. Then, Nippon Yūsen Kaisha shipped them, free of charge, aboard the NYK S.S. Awa-maru on February 14, 1912, bound for Seattle. Upon arriving at Seattle, the saplings were transferred to insulated freight cars and then headed to Washington, D.C.[69]

Photograph 14: New main building of Yokohama Nursery Company, built in 1905. *Source*: "Yokohama-ueki: 120-nen no ayumi" [120-Year History of Yokohama Nursery Company], http://www.yokohamaueki.co.jp/ayumi/index.html, accessed July 22, 2017.

Interestingly, the Yokohama Nursery Company has kept the receipt for the bill payment of ¥194.82 (currently value, about ¥750,000, or about US$7,000) for the packing and shipping of the cherry tree saplings to Yokohama port. In order to secure the health of the saplings, the company used a different method from the normal method of transporting trees. The company's former special advisor, Koizumi Shinzō, stated in February 2017: "Usually, trees are shipped with soil wrapped around their roots. But the soil contains many bacteria that could cause diseases in the plants. Therefore, we washed all the soil from the cherry tree saplings and made the saplings bare rooted. Then, we wrapped the roots of the saplings with clean sphagnum moss so that the saplings could still absorb water from their roots."[70]

Consequently, none of the 3,020 saplings that arrived in Washington, D.C. in March 1912 were diseased with bacteria or bugs. The Yokohama Nursery Company incumbent CEO/president, Ariyoshi Kazuo, stated in February 2017: "The U.S. plant quarantine personnel wrote that they were stunned to find that the saplings were shipped in impeccable condition."

Endorsing this, David Fairchild wrote that "many of the same quarantine inspectors who had examined the previous one were on hand and Doctor L. O. Howard, Chief of the Bureau of Entomology, stated that no shipment could have been cleaner and freer form insect pests."[71]

Japanese Cherry Tree Planting Ceremony

Thus, on March 26, 1912, the 3,020 Japanese cherry tree saplings arrived in Washington, D.C. safe and sound. They were hailed as a gift to the First Lady Helen Taft from the City of Tokyo. The following day, the White House held a planting ceremony at the northern end of the Tidal Basin, about 125 feet south of what is Independence Avenue, SW, today. Helen Taft, who was not fully recovered from a stroke she had suffered in 1909, planted a sapling of Somei-Yoshino. Also, Viscountess Chinda Iwa, the wife of the Japanese ambassador Chinda Sutemi, who had just assumed this assignment in Washington, D.C. a month earlier, planted another. Several officials, including Ambassador Chinda and Colonel Cosby, were present at the ceremony, whereas Scidmore was the only private citizen who attended the ceremony and stood by the first lady. There was scant publicity for the planting ceremony, but this became Helen Taft's lasting contribution as the first lady. The two original cherry trees still stand and a bronze plaque is erected at the site.[72]

Subsequently, more Somei-Yoshino saplings were planted around the Tidal Basin and the remaining Somei-Yoshino and other species of cherry trees were planted in East Potomac Park. Scidmore wrote, "The Japanese have given us their favorite,…Their own mountain flower, the soul of Japan, the symbol of all they adore and aspire to." David Fairchild recollected in 1938, "It has always seemed a pity to me that the official planting on the Speedway was not made the occasion for an elaborate ceremonial, for I do not know of any greater or more lasting instance of international friendliness than that shown by the Japanese when they sent their favorite trees to flower in the heart of our Capital." In turn, Helen Taft wrote in 1914, "I watched those that were planted later [the second consignment] with great interest and they seem to be doing very well. I wonder if any of them will ever attain the magnificent growth of the ancient and dearly loved cherry trees of Japan." She would be very pleased with what they grew to be.[73]

Concurrently with Sidmore's project in Washington, D.C., Takamine Jōkichi donated 3,000 Japanese cherry trees to New York City, for which the planting ceremony was held in front of Grant's Tomb in what is now called "Sakura Park" on April 29, 1912, with the attendance of Takamine. Then, in May 1915, in order to reciprocate in gratitude, David Fairchild made arrangements that the Department of Agriculture send several hundred dogwood trees, a large quantity of dogwood seed, and some plants of American mountain laurel to Japanese prime minister Ōkuma Shigenobu, for presentation to the City of Tokyo. This introduced the species of dogwood indigenous to North America into Japan, which is called hana-mizuki or American flowering dogwood in Japan.[74]

Former mayor of Tokyo City Ozaki Yukio visited Washington, D.C. a couple of times afterward, when the cherry blossoms were in bloom, and noted how well the cherry trees had grown. Meanwhile, he kept receiving letters and telegrams of gratitude from many people, and even received a bottle containing water from the Potomac Basin. In 1950, the 91-year old Ozaki, who was still a member of the Japanese parliament at that time, was invited by the American Council on Japan to visit New York City. He then visited Washington, D.C., where he received a resolution of appreciation by the U.S. Congress. He wrote a poem, "Watching the cherry blossoms on the Potomac, intoxicated by the moon, and admiring the snow, my life shall end." He died in October 1954, at age 95.[75]

Part IV   Scidmore and Earthquakes in Japan

18. 1896 Earthquake and Tsunami

In June 1896 (Meiji 29), a massive earthquake hit the northeastern region of Japan's main island, Honshū, with magnitude 8.2–8.5. This is known as the Meiji Sanriku Earthquake. The epicenter was off the Sanriku coast, east of Kamaishi-chō (current Kamaishi city), Iwate prefecture. Although the earthquake itself was not exceptionally strong, it caused two huge tsunamis in a row, and local residents were caught off guard. The tsunami waves reached a record height of 125.3 feet long in Ryōri Bay in current Ōfuanto, Iwate prefecture. The tsunamis destroyed and swept away a total of 11,722 houses and caused a death toll of 21,959 (including those who were missing) and 4,398 injuries. Fourteen hours later, the waves reached Hawaii, where they measured 30 feet, and then the California coast with 9.5-foot waves.[76]

Schidmore did not wait to visit the Sanriku coast and reported the widespread destruction in *National Geographic*. Her article entitled, "The Recent Earthquake Wave on the Coast of Japan," appeared in the September 1896 issue. She wrote:

On the evening of June 15, 1896, the northeast coast of Hondo, the main island of Japan, was struck by a great earthquake wave (*tsunami*), which was more destructive of life and property than any earthquake convulsion of this century in that empire. The whole coastline of the San-Riku, the three provinces of Rikuzen, Rikuchu, and Rikuoku...was laid waste by a great wave moving from the east and south,...this picturesque, fiord-cut coast is so remote and so isolated that only two foreigners had been seen in the region in ten years, with the exception of the French mission priest, Father Raspail, who lost his life in the flood...A half-demented soldier...became convinced that the first cannonading sound was from a hostile fleet, and, seizing his sword, ran down to the beach to meet the foe.[77]

Photograph 15: Meiji Sanriku Earthquake, June 1896. *Source*:

Eliza Ruhamah Scidmore, "The Recent Earthquake Wave on the

Coast of Japan," *National Geographic*, September 1896,

http://ngm.nationalgeographic.com/1896/09/japan-

tsunami/scidmore-text.

The villagers on that remote coast adhered to the old

calendar in observing their local fêtes and holidays, and on

that fifth day of the fifth moon had been celebrating the

Girls' Festival…with a rumbling as of heavy cannonading

out at sea, a roar, and the crash and crackling of timbers, they were suddenly engulfed in the swirling waters…the Wave stood like a black wall 80 feel in height, with phosphorescent lights gleaming along its crest. Others, hearing a distant roar, saw a dark shadow seaward and ran to high ground, crying "*Tsunami! tsunami!*"…all the bodies recovered were frightfully battered and mutilated, rolled over and driven against rocks, struck by and crushed between timbers.[78]

Scidmore also meticulously reported the plight of the survivors:

One loyal schoolmaster carried the emperor's portrait to a place of safety before seeking out his own family…The wave flooded the cells of Okachi prison and the jailers broke the bolts and let the 195 convicts free. Only two convicts attempted to escape, the others waiting in good order until marched to the high ground by their keepers…With houses, nets, and fishing-boats carried away and the fish retreating to further and deeper waters, starvation faced them, and, the great heat continuing while so many bodies were strewn along shore and imprisoned in ruins, the atmosphere fast became poisonous…the greater number…were suffering from pneumonia and internal inflammations consequent upon their long exposure in wet clothing without shelter and from the brine, fish oil, and sand breathed in and swallowed while in the first tumult of waters…the government has made large assignments from its available funds and sent stores of provisions, clothing, tools, etc., to the 60,000 homeless, ruined, bereaved, and starving people of the San-Riku coast.[79]

In this article, Scidmore introduced the Japanese word, *"tsunami"* (a great wave caused by an earthquake). This is considered the earliest written reference to the word *"tsunami"* in English literature. A century later, the term has gained international use, especially after the Indian Ocean Earthquake that hit off Sumatra Island and devastated Indonesia and its neighboring countries in December 2004.[80]

19. 2011 Earthquake and Tsunami

A century later, in March 2011, a massive earthquake of magnitude
9.0 hit the Sanriku region again. This time, the earthquake not
only caused huge tsunamis—with the highest being 131.6 feet in
Ryōri Bay, Ōfuanto, but also triggered the nuclear disaster of Level
7, a Major Accident on the International Nuclear Event Scale, at
the Fukushima Daiichi Nuclear Power Station, resulting in 146,520
displaced persons, as well as 18,446 deaths (including those who
were missing) and 6,152 injuries. Owing to Scidmore's reporting
in 1896, Westerners were familiar with the word *tsunami* and its
destructive power, and international support poured in the region.
Nevertheless, as of August 2017, the evacuees from Fukushima
remain displaced persons, who are called "Nuclear Disaster
Gypsies," while their children are bullied and told, "You,
Fukushima, Go back," resulting in suicide for some. In turn, the
Japanese government has cut subsidies for temporary housing of
the evacuees, in order to induce them to return to Fukushima,
claiming that it is safe to live there now. Yet, former residents no
longer trust the government, which had ensured the safety of

nuclear power stations when it built them. Consequently, they remain displaced persons in their own country.[81]

Meanwhile, the farmland in Fukushima was contaminated by radioactive substances to a gravely dangerous level, to this day. In May 2017, the level of cesium 134 and cesium 137 in the suburbs of Fukushima was 5.7 times that of restricted areas in nuclear power stations and in radiation laboratories in hospitals. However, the Japanese government has done nothing to clean up the farmland there. The excuse is that 99 percent of the farmers in Fukushima prefecture are self-employed. The farmers are in a dilemma because if they disclose the radioactive level to the public, their produce will be shut out from the market again, as in the years following the nuclear disaster. On the other hand, they are gravely concerned with the long-term effects of the contaminated soil.[82]

This is how the Japanese government is treating the industrious farmers, who for generations labored to maintain the pristine farm landscapes in the countryside that Scidmore admired. What would she have felt had she learned of the present state of the victims of the 2011 Earthquake and Tsunami?

Part V   Scidmore and Russian POWs in Japan

20. Russian POWs in Japan

In 1907, Scidmore wrote, anonymously, *As The Hague Ordains: Journal of a Russian Prisoner's Wife in Japan*, her first and only known fiction. During the Russo-Japanese War, 2,000 Japanese military personnel were captured by the Russian Army in Manchuria (Northeast China), for which sphere of interest the two countries were fighting. This number denotes that of prisoners of war (POWs), who were handed over at the time of the Portsmouth Peace Treaty, and excludes 19 POWs who died during internment in Russia. (Scidmore writes that there were 12,000 Japanese POWs in Russia.) In turn, 77,120 Russian invalids were captured by the Imperial Japanese Army (IJA) and taken to Japan for treatment from Dalian, at the tip of the Liaoning peninsula in Manchuria. In China (Qing dynasty), there were no proper medical facilities to treat the invalids.[83]

Photograph 16: Cover design of Eliza Ruhamah Scidmore's *As The Hague Ordains: Journal of a Russian Prisoner's Wife in Japan*, New York: Henry Holt, 1907.

1899 Hague Convention

As an ardent and alert journalist, Scidmore wanted to investigate how the Japanese treated Russian POWs, in the light of the Hague Convention that was signed in July 1899 and went into force in September 1900. Book IV of the convention, "Convention with Respect to the Laws and Customs of War on Land (Hague IV)" has a chapter on POWs. In addition to the general and reasonable provisions that stipulate that POWs must be humanely treated (Article 4) and that "they shall be treated as regards board, lodging, and clothing on the same footing as the troops of the Government that captured them" (Article 7), the chapter has more specific and surprisingly generous provisions. For instance, Article 10 states that "POWs may be set at liberty on parole if the laws of their country authorize it, and in such a case, they are bound, on their personal honor, scrupulously to fulfill, both as regards their own Government and the Government by whom they were made prisoners, the engagements they have contracted."[84]

Further, Article 18 provides that "POWs shall enjoy every latitude in the exercise of their religion, including attendance at their own church services, provided only they comply with the regulations for order and police issued by the military authorities." The Hague Convention was originally proposed by Russian tsar Nicholas II. Japan and Russia were among the initial 24 signatories to the convention. Then, the second Hague Convention was added in 1907.[85]

21. Visiting Russian POW Asylums in Matsuyama

Scidmore obtained permission from the Japanese Ministry of War to visit the asylums for the Russian POWs. This was an unusual measure to give to an American woman by the Japanese government, with the exception of a few volunteer nurses and missionaries. That her brother served as the legal advisor at the U.S. Legation in Tokyo during the Russo-Japanese War might have facilitated this. In 1904–1905, Russian POWs were interned in 221 asylums in 29 places throughout Japan, such as Hamadera (in Sakai, Osaka prefecture), Kyoto, Nagoya, and Narashino (in Chiba prefecture). The first asylums were created in Matsuyama, Ehime prefecture, on Shikoku Island, in remote southwestern Japan, where a total of 4,000–6,000 (depending on the source) Russian POWs were interned in the two-year period, in the town of population 30,000.[86]

Scidmore first visited the asylums in Matsuyama. The Russian POWs there were initially assigned to several local Buddhist temples until the town created a hospital with 25 (or 26) independent ward units for them. There, she found the treatment of the Russian POWs exemplary. Realizing what she had observed there involved a profound human document that was beyond the scope of a simple article or a travelogue, she transformed her account into a fiction. The result is her only known novel, *As The Hague Ordains: Journal of a Russian Prisoner's Wife in Japan* (1907). This journal began in St. Petersburg on June 16, 1904, when the protagonist learned that her husband had been captured and taken to Japan, and ends in Kobe on December 11, 1905, when the couple left Japan.[87]

22. Journal of Sophia Ivanova von Theill

The protagonist, Sophia Ivanova von Theill, decided to go to Japan, via Europe and the United States, and to visit Matsuyama where her husband Vladimir von Theill, a Russian diplomat, was interned. With the help of many people, and a luck, she managed to arrive in Matsuyama. While tending her husband and other Russian invalids under the supervision of the IJA and the Japanese Red Cross Society (JRCS), Sophia wrote a journal for one and a half years. Through Sophia's journal, Scidmore meticulously described how Russian POWs were treated by Japanese wardens, doctors and nurses, as well as by local folk in Matsuyama.[88]

For instance, Sophia writes in her journal that Russian POWs "live, two to each alcove, free to wander in and out and visit each other and go to adjoining wards, when they are able to walk. It is not my idea of a prison at all. Surely there is the fullest liberty within the barracks. There are no fetters, no restrictions. Everything is plain to a degree; simple, hygienic, and clean; and when I consider and sum up all these things, I wonder if there is anything at all to complain of. The prisoners' lot could not well be a happier one, and I, for one, would be less willing to be a prisoner-of-war in some places I can think of in Russia."[89]

Sophia tells a grudging Russian officer:

[The] Japanese feed you better in this little faraway provincial town of Matsuyama, than the Prussians could or would feed the old Comte de——in that large city of Germany…You should be living on fish and rice, pickled plums and *daikon* [Japanese radish], by the convention of The Hague…[Nevertheless,] you have good white bread—made from the most expensive American flour…soup, meat, vegetables, tea. You have clean, hot food three times a day; you have a clean bed, abundant covering and clothing, hot baths, more fresh air than you want, and a chance to walk in a narrow graveyard at any time…And so has every Cossack here.[90]

Sophia describes the scene of her meeting with Russian POWs who had just arrived in Matsuyama from Dalian after the Battle of Liaoyang (August–September 1904): "They could hardly believe that the Japanese let me stay here and tend my wounded husband daily, or that I was safe." Then, one of the POWs, who had thought that he would be killed by the Japanese when they captured him, told Sophia, "Yes! They have certainly surprised me, for they were kind to us all the time. We have been treated as their own wounded…I did not expect them to pick me up, and carry me to the surgeon, and dress my wounds; feed and fan me, put a cigarette in my mouth and light it for me. Then, a French-speaking interpreter came and asked me if I would like to go to the expense of a telegram to my family, lest they be alarmed from the Russian report of missing. It was all very strange, very surprising to me." Sophia did not respond to this, as she was certain that he was in for more surprises as the Japanese nurses were eager to take her place and take care of him.[91]

Photograph 17: A Russian POW on a stretcher smoking a cigarette
given by a Japanese soldier, Dalian, 1904. *Source*: Eliza
Ruhamah Scidmore, *As The Hague Ordains: Journal of a Russian
Prisoner's Wife in Japan*, New York, NY: Henry Holt, 1907, in
between pages 124 and 125.

23. Lafcadio Hearn and the Heart of the Japanese

Sophia was allowed to hold a music concert for the POWs and to order books for them. She found that the censorship at the internment camp was very loose and writes, "Even in war time, their Japanese temporary censorship of the press does not equal what we have in Russia in time of peace; and there are no books barred out, to judge of what was in the bookstores at Kobe; and any books we order they send us." Among many books she ordered were works of Lafcadio Hearn (June 1850–September 1904), an Irish-Greek writer who was naturalized in Japan in 1896 and assumed a Japanese name, Koizumi Yakumo. She refers to Hearn as "the one true expounder of this human mystery, Japan."[92]

By reading Hearn's *Kokoro: Hints and Echoes of Japanese Inner Life* (1896; *kokoro* literally means, "heart"), Sophia hoped that the Russians would understand why the Japanese were so altruistic and extended their hospitality toward the POWs. Interestingly, Takamine Jōkichi met Hearn in New Orleans in 1884, at the World's Industrial and Cotton Centennial Exposition. As Hearn was a newspaper reporter in the United States until he moved to Japan in 1890, Scidmore also might very well have crossed paths with Hearn, either in the United States or Japan.[93]

Hospitality of Local Folk

Sophia also writes of the hospitality of local folk in Matsuyama, "We have so many kindly little attentions from the common people, that Vladimir begins to admit much that I claim for the high soul of the race. Every few nights, a rain of cigarettes, plums, fans, and little trifles comes over the fence of the Kokaido and the Dairinji [where Russian POWs are interned]. The rain of manna, of course, pleased the Cossacks, but neither they nor the officers could understand it." An American female missionary explains to Sophia: "[This] is the Japanese way of sympathizing with the poor [POWs]…You might think these poor, hard-working people would envy the [POWs'] lives of ease, and compare their present tasks with the prisoners' leisure. But this is the Japanese way. Altruism in an object lesson…I hope that some one showers mysterious gifts on the Japanese prisoners in Russia."[94]

24. Cherry Blossoms, *Bushidō*, and the Heart of the Japanese

In early February 1905, Sophia was invited by a Japanese lady to a cherry blossom viewing of a famous cherry tree in the locale. She was surprised to find the cherry blossoms white because the cherry blossoms she had seen in Tokyo were rose-pink, and asked why they were white. Then, she was even more surprised by her host's answer: "It is because of the war. So much blood has been shed in Manchuria that even the cherry flowers are pale, without colour, this year." Sophia was overwhelmed with the fact the Japanese were still mourning the war dead—Japanese and Russian—in Manchuria at an otherwise happy occasion, and writes, "I caught my breath; the tears came. Oh! these exquisite people! What other race or nation has soul and sentiment to such degree as to feel that even the flowers are blanched at the torrents of blood that had flowed in Manchuria! What a thought! How Japanese! Ah! That Lafcadio Hearn were living!" (Hearn died in 1904.)[95]

Sophia also mentions Japanese military leaders, such as Army General Nogi Maresuke and Marshal-Admiral Tōgō

Heihachirō, and praised their spirit of *bushidō* (the way of the samurai), the strict moral creed and cult for the samurai, encompassing chivalry and honor of warriors. Among many courtesies that General Nogi showed to Russian officers, he had them retain their swords at the time of the surrender in Port Arthur in January 1905. Nogi also gave special order that no flag should be raised until Lieutenant General Anatoly Stoessel had left Port Arthur. Sophia was impressed with the nobility and chivalry of *bushidō* and shed tears. She writes, "Nogi [is the] best exponent of *bushido*. I cannot imagine Stoessel doing this, had the situation been reversed—nor Kuropatkin."[96]

In retrospect of the war, Sophia states:

If Lafcadio Hearn had but written in Russian, this war could not have been. Had the court and our intellectuals only read "*Bushido*," the war would have been prevented. We are being punished for our ignorance, that is all. The majority of Russians thought the Japanese no more than another Turcoman tribe—fish-eating heathens. That is all. This war was to be merely a hunting adventure for our Cossacks…Even in their treatment of prisoners, how wonderfully well the Japanese have managed with this great number of [POWs]…The government furnishes here as much privacy and more foreign comforts than any tourist can command in a tea house, while the rank and file are in a heaven of plenty, cleanliness, comfort, and idleness they never dreamed of before, and that contrasts sharply with the suffering, the cold, disease, and starvation of the poor French prisoners in Dresden, Magdeburg,…in Christian Germany, in 1870." (*Bushido* was written by Nitobe Inazō in 1900, examined below).[97]

Sophia's journal ends on December 11, 1905:
I have been reading to Vladimir that favourite chapter of his in "Kokoro," where in liquid prose, in language as smooth as melted velvet, Lafcadio Hearn begins so musically: "Hiogo [Hyōgo] this morning, lies bathed in a limpid magnificence of light indescribable." I look over to the massed roofs of Kobe climbing steeply to the green hills beyond, out to the soft expanse of pearl sea and the blue heavens above; and, without a sound the water eddies

around the stern, the Awaji shore slips around to our starboard side, the Sanuki mountains rise and recede, and our prison life is ended.[98]

Sophia and Vladimir had no intention of living in Russia permanently because they anticipated a more violent revolution than that which had just broken out in June 1905, and the couple were planning to emigrate to in England.[99]

25. Japanese Documents on Russian POWs in Matsuyama

Scidmore's observations of the Russian quarters in Matsuyama are endorsed by Japanese documents, which record that Russian officers received a food ration of 60 sen (¥0.6) per diem and rank-and-file soldiers 30 sen, at a time when Japanese soldiers received a food ration of 16 sen per diem. The Russians were fed with eggs and milk, and beef and English tea every day, at a time when they were luxury items for the Japanese. True to Scidmore's account, they were fed with expensive white bread, but when the Japanese found out that the Russians did not like the white bread, they hired a different baker, and eventually let the Russians bake bread for themselves. The POWs also received donations of cigarettes, food and drinks, clothing, and cash, as well as a billiard set and other pastime equipment. They were allowed to go out freely and do grocery shopping, eat out, and even watch theater performances.[100]

Photograph 18: Russian POWs in front of a theater in Matsuyama, 1904. *Source*: "Nichiro-sensō-ji no Roshia-jin horyo" (Russian POWs during the Russo-Japanese War), September 13, 2015, http://blog.livedoor.jp/nwknews/archives/4936950.html.

Moreover, Russian POWs visited local public schools and observed their classes, field days, and boat races. They were also allowed to go to Dōgo Onsen, a nationally famous hot spring resort in Matsuyama, and to go to swim at the beach in Iyo, a suburb of Matsuyama. On another occasion, they took an excursion trip to

Saihinkan, a luxurious conference hall in Iyo, riding in the first-class car of the train, and were treated with Japanese tea and sweets. Further, sympathetic townsfolk held a bicycle race for them and gave them gold and silver medals and prizes. The treatment of Russian officers was even more surprising. They were allowed to live in an independent house and to send for their wives and children to Matsuyama, just as Sophia's husband Vladimir was removed from the hospital and was allowed to live in her house and "be treated with the highest consideration."[101]

Photograph 19: Russian POWs relaxing at a Japanese inn in Dōgo

Onsen, 1904. *Source*: "Nichiro-sensō-ji no Roshia-jin horyo"

(Russian POWs during the Russo-Japanese War), September 13,

2015, http://blog.livedoor.jp/nwknews/archives/4936950.html.

26. Graves for the Russian POWs

Remarkably, the local folk in Matsuyama conducted funeral services for each of the 98 Russian POWs, who had died during internment, and created graves for them in 1905. Each of the graves faces north so that the souls of the POWs could overlook their homeland. The Japanese even organized the Russian Grave Preservation Society and conducted memorial services at the graves, as well as cleaning the graves, every month to this day, for more than 110 years. Further, Matsuyama City has hosted an annual memorial service for the Russians every March, to this day.[102]

Photograph 20: Graves for Russian POWs in Matsuyama, created in 1905. *Source*: "Nichiro-sensō-ji no Roshia-jin horyo" (Russian POWs during the Russo-Japanese War), September 13, 2015, http://blog.livedoor.jp/nwknews/archives/4936950.html.

The same is true for internment camps in other places in Japan, including Hamadera in Osaka prefecture, which created graves for the 89 Russians who had died during internment there. When Russian president Vladimir Putin visited Japan in May 2002, he dropped by at the former site of the Russian internment camp in Hamadera, which has become Hamadera Park and a residential district, and erected a memorial stone with his inscription, along with that of Japanese prime minister Koizumi Jun'ichirō.[103]

These records attest that the IJA faithfully and judiciously abided by the Hague Convention and implemented the spirit embodied in the Convention. Also, local folk received Russian POWs hospitably as if they were guests from friendly countries. Scidmore was impressed with this aspect of the Japanese dispositions and mores.

27. Russian POW Asylums in Nagoya

In addition to Matsuyama, Scidmore writes about asylums in Nagoya, in the central part of Japan, where about 3,000 Russian POWs were interned in seven Buddhist temples. The temple head priests made arrangements with the Nagoya Russian Orthodox Church and allowed POWs to attend the church services regularly and even to organize their own glee club. The Japanese archbishop of the church, Petre Shibayama Noriyuki, had a gold cross that was bestowed by the Russian Tsar Nicholas II and other memorabilia. As in Matsuyama, the POWs in Nagoya enjoyed the freedom to go out and they frequented the popular entertainment district called Ōsu. Even more, Lieutenant General Alexander "Fock" (Fok) and Lieutenant General Konstantin "Smirnoff" (Smirnov) each had the use of the archbishop's palace, with a landscape garden and tennis court, and were treated as if they were part of the archbishop's family.[104]

Photograph 21: Members of Glee Club organized by Russian POWs (sitting, the Japanese archbishop of the Nagoya Russian Orthodox Church), Nagoya, 1904. *Source*: Maria Matsushima Junko, "Nagoya Seikyōkai to Roshia: Nichiro-sensō kara 21-seiki made" (Nagoya Russian Orthodox Church and Russia: From Russo-Japanese War to the 21st Century), *Oroshia-kai kaihō*, No. 17-3, February 3, 2011, http://www.for.aichi-pu.ac.jp/~kshiro/orosia17-3.html.

Further, the Buddhist temples in Nagoya created a grave for each of the 15 POWs, who had died during internment, in the Nagoya Peace Park Cemetery and held funeral services for each of them. Then, the Nagoya Russian Orthodox Church has held an annual memorial service for them every year, to this day.[105]

The way the IJA treated the Russian POWs during the Russo-Japanese War makes a stark contrast with how the Soviet Army treated the Japanese POWs in Siberia after World War II.

28. Internment of Japanese POWs in Siberia

At the end of World War II, the Soviet Army captured 660,000–760,000 Japanese in Manchuria in August 1945, transferred them to Siberia, and had them engage in forced labor in concentration camps there for years until they were repatriated by the end of December 1956. The Soviet Army did this in spite of the Geneva Convention relative to the Treatment of Prisoners of Wars adopted in July 1929 (it was revised in 1949), which the upgraded the Hague Convention and stipulated that POWs should be expeditiously released and repatriated upon the termination of the war. The Soviet Union was not a signatory to the original 1929 Geneva Convention, but signed the 1949 revision. The Japanese POWs were provided with a bare minimum food ration—a piece of Russian black bread and thin cabbage soup—so that many succumbed to the cold and died of malnutrition or epidemic typhus. It is estimated that between 60,000 and 113,000 Japanese POWs perished in the frozen land of Siberia by the end of 1956.[106]

The way the Soviet Army treated the Japanese POWs in Siberia after World War II and the way the IJA treated the Russian

POWs during the Russo-Japanese War are marked by a 'heaven and earth' difference. The Soviet Army kept the Japanese POWs and treated them cruelly for a decade *after* the war. The Soviet authorities not only failed to reciprocate Japanese measures during the Russo-Japanese War but also repaid the hospitality with atrocity. What would Scidmore's protagonist Sophia have written in her journal had she learned of this?[107]

In one true account, when the Japanese POWs were transferred to concentration camps in Siberia in 1945, their train stopped at a station after it had passed Lake Baikal. There, an old Russian appeared and gave them a big bag of cigarettes. He said, "I was captured by the Japanese Army during the Russo-Japanese War and was sent to Kyūshū and Shikoku. The Japanese treated me very kindly and warmly." Then, he waved at the Japanese POWs until the train disappeared.[108]

Shikoku is an island where Matsuyama is located. This Russian must have had a similar experience to the officer who was given a cigarette by a Japanese soldier when he was carried on a stretcher in Dalian in September 1904, and then was sent to Matsuyama and met Sophia in *As The Hague Ordains*.

29. Scidmore and *As The Hague Ordains*

In *As The Hague Ordains*, Scidmore not only accurately chronicles the day-to-day development of the Russo-Japanese War up to the Japanese takeover of Port Arthur in January 1905, through Sophia's disappointment in Lieutenant General Anatoly Stoessel, who capitulated at the 203-Meter Hill in Port Arthur, and General Alexei Kuropatkin, who withdrew his regiment at the Battle of Liaoyang (August–September 1904) and at the Battle of Fengtian (Mukden, current Shenyang; March 1905).[109]

Also, Scidmore describes the peace conference hosted by U.S. president Theodore Roosevelt. In it looms Russian distrust of their plenipotentiary, former finance minister Sergei de Witte, as Sophia writes, "Serge de Witte yielded everything, knowing they would soon reach the *impasse* and retire[.]" "Roosevelt hit the scales with his steel wrist and left Serge de Witte dumfounded with the clumsy muddle he had made of it in the beginning." "[The] pact was concluded without De Witte paying a *sou* of the enormous indemnity he was trusted to scale down! And half of

Saghalien [Sakhalin] awarded to each country! …Dismay and indignation drove the Japanese to sullen speech or gloomy silence; and strange to say, [in Matsuyama], the Russian officers denounced De Witte more violently still."[110]

By contrast, Sophia does not stop expressing her admiration for President Roosevelt, who acted as an intermediary to end the war, and writes:

Peace of the new diplomacy! Peace as she is hammered out at the American Cronstadt! All traditions are broken with. Japan and Russia have not made peace—nor wanted it. Oh, no! That terrible American President, *Il Strenuoso*, he has made it. He wanted it, he would have it…To the amazement of all the world, to the horror of all of the old school of diplomacy, that terrible M. Roosevelt would have none of their *non possumus*…this "Steel Wrist" Roosevelt fought for peace as knights jousted of old. He struggled for peace, as if it were a football on the field. He argued for peace like Maître Labori for Dreyfus. And he won, to the amazement of the world.[111]

Sophia correctly grasped the war because she subscribed to the *Kobe Shimbun* newspaper and combed through the coverage of the war and the international reaction to the war. After all, Scidmore's elder brother was an American diplomat. She therefore made her protagonist a Russian diplomat's wife and let her speak her mind. For instance, through Sophia, Scidmore poignantly expressed the despair of the Russian POWs with the unsettling situation in their homeland, where violent anarchists were taking over, as well as their realization that they could no longer live there safely when they were repatriated.[112]

Even more remarkably, Scidmore effectively weaves into this book her vast knowledge of the state of international politics in one of the most critical times in world history—at the dawn of the Bolshevik Revolution (the Second Revolution)—and candidly expresses her opinions through her protagonist. Episodes inserted in Sophia's journal are intriguing. For instance, while being held up by the U.S. immigration inspections at the New York dock, Sophia does not overlook the double standard of America. She witnessed a company of 70 Chinese immigrants being counted off and locked up in a car, to be deported to China, "exactly as we do convicts going to Siberia." Then, the Russian consul in New York said to her, "This is the land of freedom…where they do not punish the Jews, no matter what they do." Quoting in part the remark Madame Roland had made when she saw the Statue of Liberty at the Revolution Place in Paris, on her way to the guillotine on November 8, 1973, Sophia writes, "Oh! Liberty! What crimes are committed in thy name—in America."[113]

Sophia also criticizes American critics of Russia, "who had made me blush for poor Russia, including "M. Georges [sic] Kennan." George Kennan (February 1845–May 1924) was an explorer and journalist known for his journeys in the Kamchatka and Caucasus regions of Russia. After meeting exiled dissidents in Siberia, such as Catherine Breshkovsky, the "grandmother of the Russian Revolution," Kennan became an ardent critic of Tsarist Russia, but later also criticized the Bolshevik Revolution. He was a cousin twice removed of the distinguished diplomat and historian George F. Kennan (February 1904–March 2005), who shared a birthday with him.[114]

Sophia even criticizes her fellow countryman and great writer Leo Tolstoy, as a hypocrite by calling him a "crass socialist and mischief-maker of his day" and "only a past master of *la réclame*, of the art of advertising." Referring to Tolstoy's vast estate, Sophia writes, "Hardly any village in China is as filthy, the people as ignorant and in as low a condition as in that Tula village of Yasnaya Polyana beside the country home of our great reformer and humbug, Count L. Tolstoi [*sic*]…The world gets older but learns nothing; and it cherishes delusions, and the same ones, just as it did in the time of the Greek philosophers."[115]

Now, one begins to understand why Scidmore chose the form of a novel and wrote this book anonymously, at a time when few women published a book, let alone writing a critique of the state of world affairs. Overall, this book is not only about Scidmore's observations of the Japanese treatment of the Russian POWs, but also a summation of her experiences and understanding of the Japanese people and society for more than two decades. If Sophia hoped Lafcadio Hearn's book would enlighten the Russian POWs about the inner worlds of the Japanese, Scidmore's did this for the Americans. This book is a masterpiece, a culmination of Scidmore's expertise as a journalist and writer.

Part VI   Late Years

******

30. Decorated by Japanese Emperor Mutsuhito

In July 1907, the Japanese emperor Mutsuhito bestowed medals of the Order of the Precious Crown upon 29 Americans, who had participated in the Russo-Japanese War. The list includes 10 volunteer nurses (all female) and 19 war correspondents (all male). This order was conferred on foreigners and women at that time. Dr. Anita Newcomb McGee (November 1864–October 1940), physician and founder of the Daughters of the American Revolution Hospital Corps (DAR), received the Order of the Precious Crown of the Sixth Class, while all the rest of the 28 received the Order of the Precious Crown of the Seventh Class. Interestingly, the recipients included "George Kennan of *The Outlook*" (a weekly magazine based in New York), whom Scidmore mentioned in *As the Hague Ordains*.[116]

Then, in February 1908, Scidmore was decorated with the Order of the Precious Crown of the Sixth Class by Emperor Mutsuhito for writing *As the Hague Ordains*. Her elder brother, George Hawthorne Scidmore, was decorated by the same order in 1891. Had President Abraham Lincoln learned about this, he would have been proud to know that the young siblings, for whom he had written his autograph in 1864, became respectable American citizens and accomplished great services in the Far East.[117]

After publishing *As the Hague Ordains*, Scidmore wrote no more books. Articles she wrote afterwards include: "Secrets of Forbidden Palace" (*Harper's Weekly*, February 1909); "The Cherry-Blossoms of Japan: Their Season a Period of Festivity and Poetry" (*The Century Magazine*, March 1910); "Mukden, The Manchu Home and its Great Art Museum (*National Geographic*, April 1910); "Trying to Lend China $125,000,000—A Glimpse behind the Scenes in Peking where the International Money Tournament was Fought" (*National Geographic*, May 1913); and "Young Japan" (*National Geographic*, 1914), which became her last article in *National Geographic*. Then, she was invited to give a lecture at the Japan Society of London in England that was founded in 1891 and contributed an article to its periodical entitled, "Ume no Hana, The Plum Blossom of Japan" (*Japan Society of London*, 1924). Afterwards, she stopped writing.[118]

31. Asian Exclusion Act of 1924

After the death of her brother George Scidmore in November 1922, Eliza Scidmore's life became increasingly turbulent. In April–May 1924, the U.S. Congress passed the Immigration Act of 1924, which was signed into law by President Calvin Coolidge in May 1924. This law is commonly known as the Asian Exclusion Act because it completely banned the immigration of Asians, at a time when most of the Asian immigrants were Japanese. (Chinese immigration had already been banned by the Chinese Exclusion Act of 1882, which was renewed for another ten years in 1892, and again with no terminal date in 1902.) With Japan's victory in the Russo-Japanese War, the Americans came to consider Japan a new threat and the Japanese immigration in California became a diplomatic issue between Japan and the United States.[119]

In 1913, the State of California passed the California Alien Land Law of 1913 (The Webb–Haney Act), which banned "aliens ineligible for U.S. citizenship" from owning agricultural land or possessing a long-term lease for a period of more than three years. The enactment was followed by another California Alien Land

Law of 1920, which banned a lease for a period of three years or less and forbade owning stock in companies that acquired agricultural land. These laws targeted the Japanese, as their text clearly stipulated, "The intent of the law was to restrict land ownership by Japanese immigrants. However, by assigning ownership of land to second generation children, born in the United States and thus citizens, or by the use of extended leases the law could be evaded. The result was Proposition 1 on the California ballot in 1920."[120]

In 1923, the U.S. Supreme Court upheld the two laws and determined that they were not in violation of the Fourteenth Amendment to the U.S. Constitution. Worse, the discriminatory enactments of the State of California expanded to a national scale, and the U.S. Congress passed the Immigration Act of 1917. This act implemented a literacy test in English for immigrants over 16 years old, increased the tax paid by new immigrants upon arrival, and gave immigration officials the power to exercise more discretion in making decisions over whom to exclude. The act paved the way for a new Immigration Act of 1924 (The Johnson–Reed Act), encompassing the National Origins Act and the Asian

Exclusion Act. The U.S. Congress passed it despite a gentlemen's agreement with the Japanese government, in which the latter voluntarily limited the number of Japanese emigrants by not issuing passports. The Immigration Act of 1924 shut the door to Japanese immigration to the United States altogether.[121]

Scidmore Protests the Asian Exclusion Act

The series of exclusionist enactments made people like Takamine Jōkichi, who had donated his fortune to Scidmore's cherry tree project, persona non grata in the United States. Scidmore vehemently protested the enactment of the Asian Exclusion Act, but to no avail. In despair, she decided to leave the country. In January 1925, she sold the porcelains and other art objects that she had collected in Japan and elsewhere in the Far East over the years, in order to pay for her relocation to Geneva, Switzerland. Among the artifacts she sold were the throne that Empress Dowager Cixi of the Qing dynasty in China used at the Summer Palace in Beijing. One would be hard pressed imagine the depth of the sorrow Scidmore might have felt at that time to witness the

Japanese citizens being barred from immigrating to her own country and being discriminated against in her homeland.[122]

32. Moving to Geneva and Working with Nitobe Inazō

In May 1925, Scidmore moved permanently to Geneva, Switzerland, which was the center of the international humanitarian and peace movement, with the headquarters of the International Committee of the Red Cross (ICRC) and the newly created League of Nations. Scidmore had been involved in activities of the ICRC and had attended its General Assembly in May 1912. Her beautiful apartment on the Quai de Mont Blanc, facing Lake Geneva, served as a saloon for American delegations to the League of Nations. She was also closely associated with the distinguished Japanese agronomist turned educator/diplomat, Nitobe Inazō (September 1862–October 1933), and his wife Mary (née Mary Patterson Elkinton), who was an American Quaker from Philadelphia. In Geneva, Nitobe was serving as one of the under secretaries general of the League of Nations from its inception in 1920.[123]

Photograph 22: Portrait of Nitobe Inazō on the ¥5,000 bill.

Born as the third son of the chamberlain of the lord of Mutsu province in Morioka (in current Iwate prefecture), Nitobe developed an interest in things of the West during his childhood and learned English from the family doctor. However, when Emperor Meiji dropped by at the Nitobe residence during his tour of northeast Japan, the emperor told the young Nitobe to pursue a career in agriculture as his grandfather did. Thus, Nitobe enrolled in the second graduating class of Sapporo Agricultural College (current Hokkaido University), where Massachusetts Agricultural College (current University of Massachusetts Amherst) president William S. Clark was appointed as its vice-president (president in effect). There, Clark left the young Japanese with the indelible motto, "Boys, be ambitious!," and enlightened countless Japanese, including Nitobe, who converted to Christianity. Upon graduation, Nitobe went to Tokyo Imperial University, and then transferred to Johns Hopkins University and studied economics and political science (one of his classmates was Woodrow Wilson). While in Baltimore, he joined the Religious Society of Friends and met Mary Patterson Elkinton in a Quaker community in Philadelphia, whom he married in 1891.[124]

Nitobe is most known in the English-speaking world for writing *Bushido: The Soul of Japan* (1900), describing the way of the samurai or the Japanese code of chivalry, which embodies eight virtues—rectitude, courage, benevolence, respect, integrity, honor, loyalty, and self-control. This seminal book had a great impact on such leaders as U.S. President Theodore Roosevelt, the Boy Scouts founder Robert Baden-Powell, and later, John F. Kennedy. President Roosevelt liked the book so much that he distributed copies of *Bushido* to the U.S. Army and Navy, as a textbook. Afterwards, in 1908, a Japanese translation was published.[125]

Photograph 23: Cover design of Inazo Nitobe's *Bushido: The Soul of Japan*, Philadelphia, PA: Leeds & Biddle, 1900.

At the Paris Peace Conference in 1919, Nitobe worked on the adoption of the "racial equality clause" in the Covenant of the League of Nations, submitted by the Japanese delegation. It did so because Japan had suffered from unequal treaties since it opened itself to the Western world in the 1850s. The proposal obtained a clear majority vote at the League of Nations Commission, but was vetoed by its presiding chair, U.S. president Woodrow Wilson, in recourse to a requirement for a unanimous vote. Wilson did not want to make this clause an obstacle to the ratification of the Treaty of Versailles by the U.S. Senate. In hindsight, by proposing this clause, the Japanese delegation simply tried to have the League of Nations acknowledge the equality of Japanese nationals, but failed to fathom the implications of the clause to other member countries that practiced racial inequality at home.[126]

Nitobe was also a founding director of the International Committee on Intellectual Cooperation, a prototype of the United Nations Educational, Scientific and Cultural Organization (UNESCO). Meanwhile, gravely concerned with the rise of Japanese militarism, Nitobe joined the Institute of Pacific Relations (IPR), organized in Honolulu in 1925, and created its Japan chapter. If Nitobe was disheartened by the U.S. Immigration Act of 1924, he was devastated by Japan's withdrew from the League of Nations in March 1933, in the aftermath of the creation of the Japanese puppet state in Manchuria. In October 1933, Nitobe attended a conference of the IPR held in Banff, Alberta, Canada, and on his way home, died in Victoria, Vancouver Island, where he was to embark for his voyage back.[127]

Scidmore had actually known Nitobe and his wife Mary (Mariko, her Japanese name) since 1905. In April 1905, Sidmore met Nitobe in Kyoto, where he taught at the Kyoto Imperial University Faculty of Law. Then, in January 1912, when Nitobe stayed in the United States as one of the first two exchange professors between Japan and the United States, sponsored by the Carnegie Endowment for International Peace for the academic year 1911–1912, Sidmore gave him and his wife a welcoming party at her house in Washington, D.C. Also, in April 1922, she visited Nitobe in Genthod, in the suburb of Geneva. After that, Scidmore worked closely with Nitobe and his wife for humanitarian and pacifist causes until December 1926, when Nitobe resigned his post at the League of Nations. She saw the couple off at Marseilles on their voyage home in February 1927.[128]

33. Death

On April 16, 1927, the first Washington, D.C. Cherry Blossom Festival was held, but Scidmore did not attend it. She never returned to her homeland. On November 3, 1928, she died of heart failure in her apartment at age 72. She left a will addressed to the U.S. consul in Geneva, Gibson G. Blake, specifying that no funeral service be held for her, that her body be cremated, and that her ashes be distributed in the most seemly way. However, her kin and friends decided to conduct a memorial service on November 7, to which the Japanese MOFA sent its minister (*kōshi*) in Berlin. U.S. minister in Geneva, Hugh R. Wilson, who had known both Eliza and her brother George Sidmore in person, gave a touching eulogy. Then, in accordance with her will, most of her writings were disposed of.[129]

Yokohama Foreign General Cemetery

In November 1929, at the one-year anniversary of Scidmore's death, the Japanese MOFA, as a tribute to her, made arrangements for her ashes to be interred in Lot 15 in the Yokohama Foreign

General Cemetery, where her mother Eliza Catherine Scidmore

was laid to rest in 1916. The ashes of her brother George

Hawthorne Scidmore were interred in her mother's grave in 1922.

The interment ceremony for Eliza Ruhamah Scidmore was

conducted by Yokohama Union Church minister with those

attending including the U.S. deputy ambassador, the U.S. consul,

and the English consul and his wife, as well as a representative of

the Japanese foreign minister, the Yokohama City mayor, a former

Japanese ambassador to the United States, and Nitobe Inazō and

his wife. Next to the large gravestone of her mother, Scidmore's

ashes were interred and a small memorial stone was erected.[130]

Photograph 24: Grave of the Scidmore family at the Yokohama Foreign General Cemetery (the small stone on the left is Eliza's memorial stone; the large gravestone on the right is her mother's).

Located in the scenic and historic Yamate district, the Yokohama Foreign General Cemetery is a popular tourist destination among Japanese. The cemetery overlooks Yokohama port, at which wharf the venerable NYK Hikawa-maru, the ocean liner that carried countless Japanese to the United States from her maiden voyage from Kobe to Seattle in 1930 until 1960, is permanently berthed as a museum ship. Also, countless

Americans have landed at Yokohama port since Commodore
Matthew C. Perry concluded the Japan–U.S. Peace and Amity
Treaty in March 1854 in Kanagawa, Yokohama. Now, Scidmore
rests at peace in the historic cemetery, with her mother and brother,
in a country she loved.[131]

Photograph 25: Memorial stone for Eliza Ruhamah Scidmore at
the Yokohama Foreign General Cemetery, erected November
1929. The inscription in Japanese reads: "A women who loved
Japan's *sakura* rests here."

34. Aftermath of the Japanese Cherry Trees in Washington, D.C.

In March 1935, civic groups organized the first National Cherry Blossom Festival in Washington, D.C. This became an annual event afterwards, and is celebrated every year on March 27, to this day. Thus, the Japanese cherry blossoms became a hallmark of Washington, D.C., as they came to symbolize natural splendor in the nation's capital, adding rich and colorful sights. Scidmore's vision helped to shape the public face of the nation's capital and her passion created a popular tourist spot at the heart of the United States.[132]

World War II Period

On December 11, 1941, four Japanese cherry trees at the Potomac Tidal Basin were cut down in what appeared to retaliation for the Japanese attack on Pearl Harbor, although the real circumstances for the vandalism were not substantiated. Following this, the Japanese cherry trees were referred to as "Oriental flowering cherry trees" during World War II, in order to preempt further damage to the cherry trees. In turn, the famed cherry tree grove along the Arakawa River in Adachi ward, in Tokyo, where the budwood of the Somei-Yoshino trees was taken to make saplings—which became the parent stock for the Japanese cherry trees planted around the Tidal Basin—had fallen into decline during World War II, due to the U.S. B-29s air raids on Tokyo.[133]

Post-World War II Period: "Homecoming Cherry Trees"

In 1952, Adachi ward, Tokyo, where the Arakawa River bank is located, requested U.S. government help to restore the cherry tree grove on the Arakawa River bank. In response, the U.S. National Park Service shipped budwood from descendants of the original Japanese cherry trees planted in 1912 back to Tokyo. Thus, the cherry trees that Scidmore had sent for from Japan in 1912 made a homecoming four decades later. Then, another four decades later, on March 27, 1996, a "sister river agreement" was signed between the Arakawa River and the Potomac River, affirming the enduring friendship between Japan and the United States.[134]

Meanwhile, in 1987, volunteers in Yokohama organized the Eliza Scidmore Cherry Blossom Society (Shidomoa sakura no kai) in recognition of her contributions to the friendship between Japan and the United States. Then, in 1991, the society sent for several saplings of the 1912 original Japanese cherry trees from the Potomac Tidal Basin and transplanted four of them by Scidmore's gravestone in the Yokohama Foreign General Cemetery. Thus, the descendants of the 1912 Japanese cherry trees now watch over Scidmore's grave. The society also made more graftings from the "homecoming cherry trees" at Scidmore's grave and planted them in several places in Yokohama, as of April 2012. The society hoped to plant saplings of the homecoming cherry trees all over Japan, in order to keep Scidmore's legacy alive.[135]

Usuzumi-zakura Goes to Washington, D.C.

Then, in 1999, as many as 50 propagates of the legendary 1,500-year old Usuzumi-zakura—"zakura" is *rendaku* ("sequential voicing") of "sakura," in which "s" is pronounced "z" due to the preceding word, similar to liaison in French language—were planted in West Potomac Park. It is one of the Three Grand Cherry Trees in Japan. The record has it that the 26th Japanese emperor Keitai planted an Edo-higan (a species of cherry tree that grows in the mountains) in Neodani, in current Motosu, Gifu prefecture, circa 467, as a departing gift, when he left Neodani and moved back to the capital. The poem he wrote on that occasion mentions the word "*usuzumi*," which alludes to an ephemeral life. Hence the cherry tree was named Usuzumi-zakura. In 1922, the cherry tree was designated as a Natural Monument of Japan. Then, in 1948, the tree was diagnosed to die within three years and a local tree doctor grafted a young cherry tree root onto the tree. The Usuzumi-zakura was "resuscitated" in 1950 and still stands today.[136]

Meanwhile, continuing efforts have been made by the U.S. National Park Service and the U.S. National Arboretum to preserve the genetic lineage of the original 1912 Japanese flowering cherry trees. For instance, in June 1997, cuttings were taken from the documented, surviving 1912 Somei-Yoshino trees for the purpose of propagation. Further, in 2011, about 120 propagates from the surviving 1912 Somei-Yoshino trees were sent to the Japan Cherry Blossom Society in Tokyo, in order to ensure the preservation of the trees' genetic lineage there. Then, in 2016, more cuttings were taken from the cherry trees throughout the Tidal Basin area and West Potomac Park to be propagated for preservation purposes. Through this cycle of exchanges and propagations of the 1912 parent stock, the Japanese cherry trees continue to fulfill their role as a symbol of friendship between the people of Japan and of the United States.[137]

35. Propagation of "Scidmore-zakura"

Further, in order to immortalize the friendship between Americans and Japanese that was fostered by Scidmore, a Japanese tree doctor by the name of Ikemoto Saburō in Kawawa, Yokohama, in 2016, cut branches of the "homecoming cherry trees" at Scidmore's grave in the Yokohama Foreign General Cemetery and made graftings. Kawawa is known for horticulture of chrysanthemums, as Scidmore acknowledged it in *Jinrikisha Days in Japan* (1891). She visited Kawawa 130 years ago, and not only admired the hue of the gorgeous flowers but also enjoyed a salad made of yellow chrysanthemum petals, which she called "most aesthetic of dishes."[138]

The tree doctor Ikemoto defines "Scidmore-zakura" as the successfully grafted saplings of the "homecoming cherry trees" that had grown to be more than one year old. This is not the official name of the species of the cherry tree, but a nickname. Then, in February 2017, Ikemoto and his team planted Scidmore-zakura saplings, about 4 feet in height, in Kawawa. The caretaker of the Scidmore-zakura, Kamoshida Kiyoshi, stated, "they will bloom next spring." Ikemoto added, "Five or six years from now, we can have a fine *hana-mi* [cherry blossom viewing] here. We are doing this so that the Japanese will remember that there was such a wonderful American woman who loved cherry blossoms as much as the Japanese."[139]

In addition, a new sapling was made from the "homecoming cherry trees" in the Yokohama Foreign General Cemetery and was planted in the downtown district in Yokohama, not far from the cemetery. It is located one minute's walk from Exit 5 of Ishikawa-chō (or Motomachi–Chūkagai) station of the JR (Japan Railways) Negishi Line. The signboard reads, "Scidmore-zakura," with its provenance and Scidmore's portrait photograph. Thus, the propagation of Scidmore-zakura continues as an ongoing project.[140]

36. Conclusion

Eliza Ruhamah Scidmore was a pioneering woman in many respects. She was a pioneering female international traveler and journalist/photographer. She wrote the first travel book for Alaska, ushering in the age of the Alaska cruise. She was the first female member of the Board of Trustees of the National Geographic Society. She was also the initial proponent of transplanting Japanese flowering cherry trees to Washington, D.C., which led to the annual National Cherry Blossom Festival. Moreover, she was a pioneering conservationist and spoke for the National Forest Reserves. In the end, she was a humanitarian and peace advocate and challenged the discrimination against the Japanese in her homeland.

Through her prolific writings, such as in *National Geographic* and *The Century Magazine*, she continued to enlighten Americans about exotic cultures in Asia, as well as about the significance of nature conservation. Also, her vision and passion helped to shape the public face of the nation's capital and created a popular tourist spot at the heart of the United States, where 1.5

163

million Americans visit and enjoy the spectacular view of cherry blossoms every year. Because the cherry blossoms symbolize the ephemerality of life, they make us appreciate life and nature even more profoundly and make us embrace empathy for others. As the cherry blossoms by the Potomac Tidal Basin brighten the hearts of millions of people every spring, Scidmore's legacy will live forever.

Selected Bibliography

I   Sources in English

Books

Benesch, Oleg. *Inventing the Way of the Samurai: Nationalism, Internationalism, and Bushido in Modern Japan.* Oxford: Oxford University Press, 2014.

Fairchild, David. *The World Was My Garden: Travels of a Plant Explorer.* New York: C. Scribner's Sons, 1938.

Hearn, Lafcadio. *Kokoro: Hints and Echoes of Japanese Inner Life.* Boston, MA: Houghton Mifflin, 1896.

Itoh, Mayumi. *The Making of China's Peace with Japan: What Xi Jinping Should Learn from Zhou Enlai.* New York: Palgrave McMillan, 2017.

_____. *"Hachi-ko" in Siberia: The True Story of Japanese Prisoners of War and a Dog.* Self-publication, distributed by Amazon, 2017.

Kawakami, Kiyoshi Karl. *Jokichi Takamine: A Record of His American Achievements.* New York: W.E. Rudge, 1928.

Kennan, George. *Tent Life in Siberia: Adventures Among the Koraks and Other Tribes in Kamchatka and Northern Asia.* New York: G.P. Putnam's Sons, 1870.

_____. *A Russian Comedy of Errors, With Other Stories and Sketches of Russian Life.* New York: The Century, 1915.

McClellan, Ann. *Cherry Blossoms: The Official Book of the National Cherry Blossom Festival.* Washington, D.C.: National Geographic, 2012.

_____. *The Cherry Blossom Festival: Sakura Celebration.* Piemont, NH: Bunker Hill, 2013.

Newberry Library. ed. *Report of the Trustees of the Newberry Library for the Year 1912*. Chicago, IL: Newberry Library, 1912.

Nitobe, Inazo. *Bushido: The Soul of Japan*. Philadelphia, PA: Leeds & Biddle, 1900.

Ozaki, Yukio. *The Autobiography of Ozaki Yukio: The Struggle for Constitutional Government in Japan*. Trans. by Hara Fujiko. Princeton, NJ: Princeton University Press, 2001.

Samuels, Richard J. *Rich Nation, Strong Army: National Security and the Technological Transformation of Japan*. Ithaca, NY: Cornell University Press, 1994.

Scidmore, Eliza Ruhamah. *Alaska, Its Southern Coast and the Sitkan Archipelago*. Boston, MA: D. Lothrop, 1885.

_____. *Westward to the Far East: A Guide to the Principal Cities of China and Japan.* Calgary, Alberta: Canadian Pacific Railway, 1891.

_____. *Jinrikisha Days in Japan.* New York: Harper & Brothers, 1891.

_____. *Appleton's Guide-Book to Alaska and the Northwest Coast: Including the Shores of Washington, British Columbia, Southeastern Alaska, the Aleutians and the Seal Islands, the Bering and the Arctic Coasts.* New York: D. Appleton, 1893.

_____. *Java, the Garden of the East.* New York: The Century, 1897.

_____. *China, the Long-Lived Empire.* New York: The Century, 1900.

_____. *Winter India.* New York: The Century, 1903.

_____. *As The Hague Ordains: Journal of a Russian Prisoner's Wife in Japan*. New York: Henry Holt, 1907.

Scidmore, George Hawthorne. *Outline Lectures on the History, Organization, Jurisdiction, and Practice of the Ministerial and Consular Courts of the Unites States of America in Japan*. Making of Modern Law: Foreign, Comparative, and International Law, 1620–1926 series. Farmington, MI: Gale, 2013 (originally published in 1887).

Shurtleff, William and Aoyagi, Akiko. eds. *Jokichi Takamine (1854–1922) and Caroline Hitch Takamine (1866– 1954): Biography and Biography*. Lafayette, CA: Soyinfo Center, 2012, http://www.soyinfocenter.com/pdf/155/Taka.pdf.

Taft, Helen Herron. *Recollections of Full Years*. New York: Dodd, Mead, 1914.

Takashima, Suteta. *Illustrations of Japanese Life*. Tokyo: Ogawa Kazumasa Photo Studio, 1896.

Zimmerman, Andrea. *Eliza's Cherry Trees: Japan's Gift to America.* Illustration by Ju-Hong Chen. New York: Pelican Publishing, 2011.

Journal Articles and Selected Online and Other Publications

American Consular Bulletin, Vol. 3, No. 1, March 1921, 175.

Cooper, Rachel. "Everything to Know about the Washington, D.C. Cherry Trees." March 25, 2017, https://www.tripsavvy.com/about-the-washington-dc-cherry-trees-1038531.

Crozier, William. "Services in Memory of Eliza Ruhamah Schidmore, Held in Geneva, Switzerland, on Wednesday, November 7, 1928, at the American Church." *Pamphlets in American History*, 1988.

"Eliza Ruhamah Scidmore Photographs relating to Japan and China, circa 1914–1916."
http://sova.si.edu/record/NAA.PhotoLot.139http://sova.si.edu/record/NAA.PhotoLot.139http://collections.si.edu/search/results.htm?q=record_ID:siris_arc_2907, accessed July 2, 2017.

"Eliza Scidmore." July 6, 2016,
https://www.nps.gov/articles/eliza-scidmore.htm.

"Eliza's Life." http://www.elizascidmore.com/eliza-s-life, accessed July 2, 2017.

"Eliza's Plan." http://www.elizascidmore.com/eliza-s-plan, accessed July 2, 2017.

"Hanamai (Flower-Picnic)."
http://www.baxleystamps.com/litho/ogawa/ogawa_hanami.shtml, accessed July 21, 2017. From Takashima Suteta, *Hanamai* (*Flower Picnic*). Tokyo: Ogawa Kazumasa Photo Studio, 1897.

"History of the Cherry Trees."

https://www.nps.gov/subjects/cherryblossom/history-of-the-cherry-

trees.htm, accessed July 16, 2017.

"History of Tsunami: The Word And the Wave." "Morning

Edition," National Public Radio, March 18, 2011,

http://www.npr.org/2011/03/18/134600508/history-of-tsunami-the-

word-and-the-wave.

"Laws of War: Laws and Customs of War on Land (Hague II),

July 29, 1899," 2008,

http://avalon.law.yale.edu/19th_century/hague02.asp, accessed

July 30, 2017.

"Mikado Honors Americans: Order of the Crown Bestowed on

Nurses and War Correspondents." *The New York Times*, July 4,

1907.

"Miss Eliza Scidmore Dies in Geneva at 72: Author of 'Jinrikisha Days in Japan' and Other Books of the Far East." *The New York Times*, November 4, 1928.

"National Geographic." https://www.nationalgeographic.org, accessed July 2, 2017.

Neville, Edwin L. "George Hawthorne Scidmore." *American Consular Bulletin*, Vol. V, No. 2, February 1923, 33-35, 56-58, 60-62, http://www.afsa.org/sites/default/files/fsj-1923-02-february_0.pdf.

"Oberlin College & Conservatory," https://www.oberlin.edu, accessed July 2, 2017.

"Portsmouth Peace Treaty: 1905–2005," http://www.portsmouthpeacetreaty.org, accessed July 21, 2017.

Ruane, Michael E. "D.C.'s Cheery Blossoms and the Sad Story of Japanese Family." March 26, 2010,

http://www.washingtonpost.com/wp-

dyn/content/article/2010/03/24/AR2010032401725.html.

_____. "Cherry Blossom's Champion, Eliza Scidmore, Led a

Life of Adventure." March 13, 2012,

https://www.washingtonpost.com/local/cherry-blossoms-

champion-eliza-scidmore-led-a-life-of-

adventure/2012/02/22/gIQAAzHEAS_story.html?utm_term=.5b7b

c1c8e699.

"Sakura Park." https://www.nycgovparks.org/parks/sakura-

park/history, accessed July 23, 2017.

Scidmore, Daniel Howard. "Eliza Ruhanah Scidmore: More Than

A Footnote in History." M.A.L.S. Benedictine University, Lisle,

Illinois, thesis, approved May 2000.

Scidmore, Eliza Ruhamah. "The Recent Earthquake Wave on the

Coast of Japan." *National Geographic*, September 1896,

http://ngm.nationalgeographic.com/1896/09/japan-tsunami/scidmore-text.

_____. "Our National Forest Reserves." *The Century Magazine*, September 1893.

_____. "The Cherry-Blossoms of Japan: Their Season a Period of Festivity and Poetry." *The Century Magazine*, Vol. LXXIX, No. 5, March 1910.

"Scidmore, Eliza Ruhamah." *Who's Who in America*, Vol. 5, 1676.

"Scidmore, George Hawthorne," *Who's Who in America*, Vol. 5, 1676.

Snipes, Samuel M. "The Life of Japanese Quaker Inazo Nitobe." August 1, 2011, https://www.friendsjournal.org/life-japanese-quaker-inazo-nitobe-1862-1933/.

"The Geneva Conventions of 1949 and Their Additional

Protocols."

https://www.icrc.org/eng/war-and-law/treaties-customary-

law/geneva-

conventions/overview-geneva-conventions.htm, accessed May 15,

2017.

"The History of Enzyme Supplements."

http://deerlandenzymes.com/swallow/the-

history-of-enzyme-supplements/, accessed July 23, 2017.

"The Immigration Act of 1924 (The Johnson–Reed Act)."

https://history.state.gov/milestones/1921-1936/immigration-act,

accessed July 31, 2017.

"The Story of Cherry Blossom Trees that Served as Bridge

between Japan and the US: Cherry Blossom Tree Donation 100th

Anniversary," April 1, 2012–May 31, 2012, No. 122,

http://www.city.yokohama.lg.jp/naka/english/nwtn/nwtn2012/122.
pdf.

"Webb–Haney Alien Land Act, California, 1913."
http://www.intimeandplace.org/Japanese%20Internment/reading/c
onstitution/alienlandlaw.html, accessed July 31, 2017.

"Yokohama Foreign General Cemetery," http://www.yfgc-
japan.com/history_e.html, accessed May 31, 2017.

II Sources in Japanese

Books

Hokkoku Shimbunsha shuppankyoku. ed. *Samkurai kagakusha,*
Takamine Jōkichi (Samurai Chemist, Takamine Jōkichi).
Kanazawa: Hokkoku Shimbunsha shuppankyoku (Jishōsha-
shinsho), 2011.

Iinuma, Kazumasa and Kan'no, Tomio. *Takamine Jōkichi no shōgai: Adorenarin hakken no shinjitsu* (Life of Takamine Jōkichi: Truth about the Discovery of Adrenalin). pbk. Tokyo: Asahi-shuppan, 2000.

Kusahara, Katsuhide. *Nitobe Inazō, 1862–1933: Ware, Taiheihō no hashi to naran* (Nitobe Inazō, 1862–1933: I Shall be a Bridge over the Pacific Ocean). Tokyo: Fujiwara-shoten, 2012.

Ozaki, Gakudō (Ozaki, Yukio). *Gakudō kaikoroku* (Memoires of Ozaki Gakudō). 2 vols. Tokyo: Ondorisha, 1951.

Ozaki Gakudō zenshū hensan-iinkai. ed. *Ozaki Gakudō zenshū* (Complete Works of Ozaki Gakudō). 12 vols. Tokyo: Kōronsha, 1955–1956.

Scidmore, Eliza Ruhamah. *Nihon · Jinrikisha ryojō* (Japan: Journeys by Rickshaw; a Japanese translation of Scidmore's *Jinrikisha Days in Japan*). Trans. by Onchi Mitsuo. Yokohama: Yūrindō, 1987.

_____. *Nichiro-sensō-ka no Nihon: Roshia gunjin horyo no tsuma no nikki* (Japan during Russo-Japanese War: Journal of a Russian Prisoner's Wife in Japan; a Japanese translation of Scidmore's *As The Hague Ordains*). Trans. by Ogiso Ryū and Ogiso Miyoko. Tokyo: Shin-jinbutsu-ōraisha, 1991.

_____. *Shidomoa Nihon kikō: Meiji no jinrikisha tsuā* (Scidmore's Journeys in Japan: Rickshaw Tour in the Meiji Period; a Japanese translation of Scidmore's *Jinrikisha Days in Japan*). Trans. by Tonosaki Katsuhisa. Tokyo: Kōdansha, 2002.

Tonosaki, Katsuhisa. *Potomac no sakura: Tsugaru no gaikōkan Chinda fusai monogatari* (Cherry Blossoms at the Potomac: Tale of a Diplomat from Tsugaru, Chinda [Sutemi] and his Wife [Iwa]). Tokyo: Saimaru-shuppankai, 1994.

_____. *Potomac no sakura-monogatari: Taiheiyō no niji to naran* (Tale of Cherry Blossoms at the Potomac: I Shall be a Rainbow over the Pacific Ocean). Suwa: Chōeisha, 1998.

Un'no, Yutaka. *Potomac no sakura-monogatari:* *Sakura to*

heiwa-gaikō (Tale of Cherry Blossoms at the Potomac: Cherry

Blossoms and Peace Diplomacy). Tokyo: Gakubunsha, 2017.

Book Chapters, Journal Articles, and Selected Online

Publications

"Eliza Ruhamah Scidmore: Jinrikisha Days in Japan." June 17,

2017, https://blogs.yahoo.co.jp/mitch68canada/739333.html.

Fujisaki, Ichirō. "Sakura to gaikōkan: Washington no sakura 100-

nen ni yosete" (Cherry Blossoms and [Japanese] Diplomats: On

the Occasion of the Centennial of the Cherry Blossoms in

Washington, D.C.). March 16, 2012,

http://gyosei.47news.jp/47topics/226712php, or

https://blogs.yahoo.co.jp/kangno10212001/12830872.html.

"Hamadera horyo-shūyojō" (POW Internment Camp in

Hamadera). *Sankei Shimbun*, July 27, 2013,

http://www.sankei.com/west/news/130727/wst1307270065-n3.html.

"Hanami ga 100-bai tanoshimeri! Sakura o meguru monogatari" (Tales of Cherry Blossoms that Will Make You Enjoy Cherry Blossom Viewing 100 Times More). "Sekai fushigi hakken!," uploaded March 19, 2017, https://www.youtube.com/watch?v=DmNxSgWOXls.

Hasegawa Yūichi. "'Hainichi imin-hō' to Manshū · Burajiru" ("Japanese Exclusion Act" and Manchuria · Brazil). In Miwa Kimidata, ed., *Nichibei kiki no kigen to Hainichi imin-hō* (Origin of U.S.-Japanese Crisis and the Japanese Exclusion Act), Tokyo: Ronsōsha, 1997, 44-79.

Kita, Yoshito. "Nichiro-sensō to jindō-shugi: Matsuyama furyo-shūyōjo ni okeru Roshia shōbyōsha kyūgo no kentō" (Russo-Japanese War and Humanitarianism: Study of Relief Measures for Russian Invalids in the Matsuyama Asylum for POWs). 333

(591)-369 (627), http://www.law.nihon-u.ac.jp/publication/pdf/nihon/80_2/10.pdf, accessed July 1, 2017.

Matsushima, Maria Junko. "Nagoya Seikyōkai to Roshia: Nichiro-sensō kara 21-seiki made" (Nagoya Russian Orthodox Church and Russia: From Russo-Japanese War to the 21st Century). *Oroshia-kai kaihō*, No. 17-3, February 3, 2011, http://www.for.aichi-pu.ac.jp/~kshiro/orosia17-3.html.

"Matsuyama no kioku" (Memory of Matsuyama). April 28, 2009, http://seitousikan.blog130.fc2.com/blog-entry-373.html.

"Matsuyama-shimin no Roshia-hei horyo ni taisuru 'o-mo-te-na-shi'" (Hospitality toward Russian POWs by Matsuyama Citizens). http://dayzi.com/a-izinkatuta2.html, accessed August 1, 2017.

"Mine no hana-oru shō-daitoku: Futatabi Shidomoa-joshi ni tsuite (Regarding Miss Scidmore Again: The Small Virtue of Cutting Cherry Blossom Branches at the Mountain Peak). March 26, 2009, https://madenokouji.wordpress.com/2009/03/26/.

"Neodani Usuzumi-sakura."

http://www.city.motosu.lg.jp/sight/usuzumi/, accessed July

31, 2017.

"Nichi-bei sakura kizō 100-shūnen" (100-year Anniversary of

Cherry Tree Gift from Japan to the United States).

http://www.ny.us.emb-japan.go.jp/jp/h/245.html, accessed July 20,

2017.

"Nichiro-sensō no, Nihonjin horyo" (Japanese POWs during the

Russo-Japanese War).

http://www.rose.ne.jp/~ooha/horyo.htm, accessed July 31, 2017.

"Omona tsunami higai no gaiyō" (Overview of Damage by Major

Tsunamis). March 2005,

http://www.bousai.go.jp/jishin/tsunami/hinan/1/pdf/2.pdf.

"Roshia-hei bochi" (Cemetery for Russian Soldiers), January 20,

2017,

https://www.city.matsuyama.ehime.jp/kurashi/kurashi/bochi_nouk
otsudo/russian_soldiers.html.

"Saigai-shi ni manabu" (Lessons to be Learned from History of
Disasters). March 2011,
http://www.bousai.go.jp/kyoiku/kyokun/kyoukunnokeishou/pdf/sai
gaishi_kaikoujishin_tsunami.pdf.

"Shidomoa-zakura towa?: Eliza to Potomac-kahan no Zenbei
sakura-matsuri ni tsuite" (What is Scidmore-zakura?: Regarding
Eliza and National Cheery Blossom Festival at the Potomac).
March 18, 2017, http://medigaku.com/eliza-r-scidmore/.

"Washinton no sakura to Shidomoa-joshi no Nihon eno atsuki
omoi" (Cherry Blossoms in Washington and Passion of Miss
Scidmore for Japan). March 24, 2009,
https://madenokouji.wordpress.com/2009/03/24/.

"Yokohama-ueki: 120-nen no ayumi" (120-Year History of
Yokohama Nursery Company),

http://www.yokohamaueki.co.jp/ayumi/index.html, accessed July

22, 2017.

About the author

Mayumi Itoh is a former Professor of Political Science at the University of Nevada, Las Vegas (UNLV). She has also taught at Princeton University and Queens College, City University of New York (CUNY), and has written 15 single-authored books, as well as more than 15 articles in professional journals. Her book titles include:

–*Globalization of Japan: Japanese Sakoku Mentality and U.S. Efforts to Open Japan* (1998)

–*The Hatoyama Dynasty: Japanese Political Leadership Through the Generations* (2003)

–*Japanese War Orphans in Manchuria: Forgotten Victims of World War II* (2010)

–*Japanese Wartime Zoo Policy: The Silent Victims of World War II* (2010)

–*The Origin of Ping-Pong Diplomacy: The Forgotten Architect of Sino-U.S. Rapprochement* (2011)

–*Pioneers of Sino-Japanese Relations: Liao and Takasaki* (2012)

–*Hachi: The Truth of the Life and Legend of the Most Famous Dog in Japan* (2013)

–*The Origins of Contemporary Sino-Japanese Relations: Zhou Enlai and Japan* (2016)

–*The Making of China's War with Japan: Zhou Enlai and Zhang Xueliang* (2016)

–*The Making of China's Peace with Japan: What Xi Jinping Should Learn from Zhou Enlai* (2017)

–*"Hachi-ko" in Siberia: The True Story of Japanese Prisoners of War and a Dog* (2017)

–*Hachiko: Solving Twenty Mysteries about the Most Famous Dog in Japan* (2017)

–*Kaneko Misuzu: Life and Poems of A Lonely Princes* (forthcoming 2018)

–*The Japanese Culture of Mourning Whales: Whale Graves and Memorial Monuments in Japan* (forthcoming 2018)

–*Animals and the Fukushima Nuclear Disaster: Innocent Victims Left Behind in the Radioactive Exclusion Zone* (forthcoming 2018).

Notes

---

[1] "History of the Cherry Trees,"

https://www.nps.gov/subjects/cherryblossom/history-of-the-cherry-trees.htm, accessed July 16, 2017. For details, see also McClellan, Ann, *Cherry Blossoms: The Official Book of the National Cherry Blossom Festival*, Washington, D.C.: National Geographic, 2012 and Rachel Cooper, "Everything to Know about the Washington, D.C. Cherry Trees," March 25, 2017, https://www.tripsavvy.com/about-the-washington-dc-cherry-trees-1038531.

[2] Ibid.

[3] Books written by Eliza Ruhamah Scidmore include *Alaska, Its Southern Coast and the Sitkan Archipelago*, Boston, MA: D. Lothrop, 1885; *Westward to the Far East: A Guide to the Principal Cities of China and Japan*, Calgary, Alberta: Canadian Pacific Railway, 1891; *Jinrikisha Days in Japan*, New York: Harper & Brothers, 1891; *Appleton's Guide-Book to Alaska and the Northwest Coast: Including the Shores of Washington, British Columbia, Southeastern Alaska, the Aleutians and the Seal Islands, the Bering and the Arctic Coasts*, New York: D. Appleton, 1893;

Java, the Garden of the East, New York: The Century, 1897;

China, the Long-Lived Empire, New York: The Century, 1900;

Winter India, New York: The Century, 1903; *As The Hague*

Ordains: Journal of a Russian Prisoner's Wife in Japan, New

York: Henry Holt, 1907.

[4] "Scidmore, Eliza Ruhamah," *Who's Who in America*, Vol. 5,

1676; "Eliza's Life," http://www.elizascidmore.com/eliza-s-life,

accessed July 2, 2017. Some sources record that she was born in

Madison, Wisconsin, but the Iowa Census taken in 1856 recorded

that her family lived in Clinton, Iowa, in that year. Also, her

passport applications recorded that she was born in Clinton, Iowa.

[5] Newberry Library, ed., *Report of the Trustees of the Newberry*

Library for the Year 1912, Chicago, IL: Newberry Library, 1912,

19.

[6] "Eliza's Life."

[7] Eliza Ruhamah Scidmore, *Shidomoa Nihon kikō: Meiji no*

jinrikisha tsuā (Scidmore's Journeys in Japan: Rickshaw Tour in

the Meiji Period; a Japanese translation of Scidmore's *Jinrikisha*

Days in Japan), trans. by Tonosaki Katsuhisa, Tokyo: Kōdansha,

2002, 468; "Oberlin College & Conservatory,"

https://www.oberlin.edu, accessed July 2, 2017; "Ōbirin daikaku" (its official English name, J. F. Oberlin University), http://www.obirin.ac.jp, accessed July 2, 2017.

[8] Eliza's Life"; "Eliza Ruhamah Scidmore (2002, trans. by Tonosaki), 468; "Eliza Scidmore," July 6, 2016, https://www.nps.gov/articles/eliza-scidmore.htm.

[9] "Eliza Scidmore."

[10] Ibid.

[11] Ibid.; "Trump Will Withdraw U.S. from Paris Climate Agreement," *New York Times,* June 2, 2017.

[12] "Scidmore, George Hawthorne," *Who's Who in America*, Vol. 5, 1676; *American Consular Bulletin*, Vol. 3, No. 1, March 1921, 175; Edwin L. Neville, "George Hawthorne Scidmore," *American Consular Bulletin*, Vol. V, No. 2, February 1923, 33-35, 56-58, 60-62, http://www.afsa.org/sites/default/files/fsj-1923-02-february_0.pdf.

[13] Ibid. (all three).

[14] Ibid. (all three).

[15] Ibid. (all three); George Hawthorne Scidmore, *Outline Lectures on the History, Organization, Jurisdiction, and Practice of the*

Ministerial and Consular Courts of the Unites States of America in Japan, Making of Modern Law: Foreign, Comparative, and International Law, 1620–1926 series, Farmington, MI: Gale, 2013 (originally published in 1887); "Eliza Ruhamah Scidmore (2002, trans. by Tonosaki), 468-474.

[16] "Eliza's Life"; "Eliza Ruhamah Scidmore Photographs relating to Japan and China, circa 1914–1916," http://sova.si.edu/record/NAA.PhotoLot.139http://sova.si.edu/record/NAA.PhotoLot.139http://collections.si.edu/search/results.htm?q=record_ID:siris_arc_2907, accessed July 2, 2017; "National Geographic," https://www.nationalgeographic.org, accessed July 2, 2017.

[17] Eliza Ruhamah Scidmore (2002, trans. by Tonosaki), 468-469; "Eliza Scidmore."

[18] For details, see Richard J. Samuels, *Rich Nation, Strong Army: National Security and the Technological Transformation of Japan*, Ithaca, NY: Cornell University Press, 1994.

[19] Eliza Ruhamah Scidmore (2002, trans. by Tonosaki), 468-474.

[20] Eliza Ruhamah Scidmore, *Jinrikisha Days in Japan*, 1; Eliza Ruhamah Scidmore (2002, trans. by Tonosaki), 468-469.

[21] Ibid., 33-34; "Hanami ga 100-bai tanoshimeri! Sakura o meguru monogatari" (Tales of Cherry Blossoms that Will Make You Enjoy Cherry Blossom Viewing 100 Times More), "Sekai fushigi hakken!," uploaded March 19, 2017, https://www.youtube.com/watch?v=DmNxSgWOXls.

[22] Eliza Ruhamah Scidmore, *Jinrikisha Days in Japan*, 1, 11-12.

[23] Ibid., 1-2; Mary Norton, *The Borrowers*, London: J. M. Dent, 1952.

[24] Eliza Ruhamah Scidmore, *Jinrikisha Days in Japan*.

[25] Eliza Ruhamah Scidmore (2002, trans. by Tonosaki), preface.

[26] Eliza Ruhamah Scidmore, *Jinrikisha Days in Japan*, 3-4.

[27] Ibid., 175-181.

[28] Ibid., 181-186.

[29] Ibid., 69-70.

[30] "Hanami ga 100-bai tanoshimeri!...."

[31] Eliza Ruhamah Scidmore, *Jinrikisha Days in Japan*, 70.

[32] Ibid., 70-74.

[33] Zhou Enlai, *Zhou Enlai zaoqi wenji* 1912.10–1924.6 (Early Writings of Zhou Enlai 1912.10–1924.6). Edited by Zhonggong-zhongyang wenxian-yanjiushi and Nankai-daxue, Tianjin:

Zhonggyang wenxian-chubanshe and Nankai-daxue chubanshe, 1998, Vol. 1, 412-415.

[34] Eliza Ruhamah Scidmore, "The Cherry-Blossoms of Japan: Their Season a Period of Festivity and Poetry," *The Century Magazine*, Vol. LXXIX, No. 5, March 1910.

[35] "History of the Cherry Trees"; Fujisaki Ichirō, "Sakura to gaikōkan: Washington no sakura 100-nen ni yosete" (Cherry Blossoms and [Japanese] Diplomats: On the Occasion of the Centennial of the Cherry Blossoms in Washington, D.C.), March 16, 2012, http://gyosei.47news.jp/47topics/226712php, and https://blogs.yahoo.co.jp/kangno10212001/12830872.html.

[36] "History of the Cherry Trees"; Eliza Ruhamah Scidmore, "Our National Forest Reserves" *The Century Magazine*, September 1893; "The Story of Cherry Blossom Trees that Served as a Bridge between Japan and the US: Cherry Blossom Tree Donation 100th Anniversary," April 1, 2012–May 31, 2012, http://www.city.yokohama.lg.jp/naka/english/nwtn/nwtn2012/122.pdf.

[37] "History of the Cherry Trees"; "Eliza's Plan"; Helen Herron Taft, *Recollections of Full Years*, New York: Dudd, Mead, 1914,

52-90.

[38] Taft, 274-275, 312-313, 316.

[39] Ibid., 74-75.

[40] Ibid., 74; Michael E. Ruane, "Cherry Blossom's Champion, Eliza Scidmore, Led a Life of Adventure," March 13, 2012, https://www.washingtonpost.com/local/cherry-blossoms-champion-eliza-scidmore-led-a-life-of-adventure/2012/02/22/gIQAAzHEAS_story.html?utm_term=.5b7b c1c8e699.

[41] Taft, 361-362.

[42] "History of the Cherry Trees."

[43] Ibid.; Taft, 362.

[44] "Eliza's Plan," http://www.elizascidmore.com/eliza-s-plan; David Fairchild, *The World Was My Garden: Travels of a Plant Explorer*, New York: C. Scribner's Sons, 1938, 1-17.

[45] Fairchild, 18-29.

[46] Ibid., 212-214.

[47] Ibid., 253-254, 262.

[48] Ibid., 410-412; "History of the Cherry Trees."

[49] Kiyoshi Karl Kawakami, *Jokichi Takamine: A Record of His*

American Achievements, New York: W.E. Rudge, 1928, 13-21;

William Shurtleff and Akiko Aoyagi, eds., *Jokichi Takamine*

(1854–1922) and Caroline Hitch Takamine (1866– 1954):

Biography and Biography, Lafayette, CA: Soyinfo Center, 2012,

http://www.soyinfocenter.com/pdf/155/Taka.pdf; "The History of

Enzyme Supplements," http://deerlandenzymes.com/swallow/the-

history-of-enzyme-supplements/, accessed July 23, 2017.

[50] Kawakami, 22-51; "The History of Enzyme Supplements."

[51] Kawakami, 52-58; Shurtleff and Aoyagi.

[52] Kawakami, x, 52-62; Shurtleff and Aoyagi.

[53] "Sakura Park," https://www.nycgovparks.org/parks/sakura-

park/history, accessed July 23, 2017; "Sakura Park,"

http://www.ny.us.emb-japan.go.jp/150th/html/nyepiE2c.htm,

accessed July 23, 2017; Shurtleff and Aoyagi.

[54] "History of the Cherry Trees"; Fujisaki; Taft, 362.

[55] Ozaki Gakudō zenshū hensan-iinkai, ed., *Ozaki Gakudō zenshū*

(Complete Works of Ozaki Gakudō), 12 vols., Tokyo: Kōronsha,

1955–1956; Ozaki Yukio, *The Autobiography of Ozaki Yukio: The*

Struggle for Constitutional Government in Japan, trans. by Hara

Fujiko, Princeton, NJ: Princeton University Press, 2001, 231-232.

[56] "Portsmouth Peace Treaty: 1905–2005,"
http://www.portsmouthpeacetreaty.org, accessed July 21, 2017;
"Wentworth by the Sea,' http://www.wentworth.com/about-
us/wentworth-history/, accessed July 21, 2017.

[57] Ozaki (2001), 231-232.

[58] "History of the Cherry Trees"; Fujisaki; "Nichi-bei sakura kizō
100-shūnen" (100-year Anniversary of Cherry Tree Gift from
Japan to the United States), http://www.ny.us.emb-
japan.go.jp/jp/h/245.html, accessed July 20, 2017.

[59] "History of the Cherry Trees"; Fairchild, 412-413.

[60] Fairchild, 412-413.

[61] Ibid., 413.

[62] Ozaki, 232.

[63] Fujisaki.

[64] Ozaki, 232.

[65] Fujisaki.; "History of the Cherry Trees"; "Nichi-bei sakura kizō
100-shūnen."

[66] Fujisaki.; "History of the Cherry Trees."

[67] Fairchild, 414C, 415.

[68] Ibid., 413; Ozaki, 232.

[69] "History of the Cherry Trees"; "The Story of Cherry Blossom Trees that Served…"; "Yokohama-ueki: 120-nen no ayumi" (120-Year History of Yokohama Nursery Company), http://www.yokohamaueki.co.jp/ayumi/index.html, accessed July 22, 2017.

[70] "Hanami ga 100-bai tanoshimeri!…."

[71] Ibid.; Fairchild, 413-414.

[72] "History of the Cherry Trees"; Ruane; Fairchild, 414.

[73] Ibid. (all three); Taft, 362-363.

[74] Eliza Ruhamah Scidmore (2002, trans. by Tonosaki), 473; History of the Cherry Trees"; Fairchild, 414.

[75] Ozaki, 223, 233; Fujisaki.

[76] "Omona tsunami higai no gaiyō" (Overview of Damage by Major Tsunamis), March 2005, http://www.bousai.go.jp/jishin/tsunami/hinan/1/pdf/2.pdf; "Saigai-shi ni manabu" (Lessons to be Learned from History of Disasters), March 2011, http://www.bousai.go.jp/kyoiku/kyokun/kyoukunnokeishou/pdf/saigaishi_kaikoujishin_tsunami.pdf. For details, see Yoshimura Akira, Sanriku-kaigan Ōtsunami (Massive Tsunami on Sanriku

Coast), Tokyo: Bungei-shunjū, 2004.

[77] Eliza Ruhamah Scidmore, "The Recent Earthquake Wave on the Coast of Japan," September 1896, http://ngm.nationalgeographic.com/1896/09/japan-tsunami/scidmore-text.

[78] Ibid.

[79] Ibid.

[80] History of Tsunami: The Word And the Wave," "Morning Edition," National Public Radio, March 18, 2011, http://www.npr.org/2011/03/18/134600508/history-of-tsunami-the-word-and-the-wave.

[81] "Tokyo-denryoku Fukushima genshiryoku hatsudenjo jiko chōsa-iinkai hōkokusho" (Report of Investigation Committee for Tokyo Electric Power Company Fukushima Nuclear Power Station Accident), July 5, 2012, http://warp.da.ndl.go.jp/info:ndljp/pid/3856371/naiic.go.jp/blog/reports/main-report/reserved/4th-1/; "Fukushima hinan-ijime 199-ken" (199 Cases of Bullying of Fukushima Evacuees), *Tokyo Shimbun*, April 11, 2017.

[82] "Nōchi no hōshano osen taisaku okizari" ([Japanese

Government] Has Ignored Taking Measures to Clean Up Radioactive Contamination of Farmland), *Tokyo Shimbun*, July 4, 2017.

[83] Eliza Ruhamah Scidmore (1907), 305; "Nichiro-sensō no, Nihonjin horyo" (Japanese POWs during the Russo-Japanese War), http://www.rose.ne.jp/~ooha/horyo.htm, accessed July 31, 2017.

[84] "Laws of War: Laws and Customs of War on Land (Hague II), July 29, 1899," 2008, http://avalon.law.yale.edu/19th_century/hague02.asp, accessed July 30, 2017.

[85] Ibid.

[86] Eliza Ruhamah Scidmore (1907); Kita Yoshito, "Nichiro-sensō to jindō-shugi: Matsuyama furyo-shūyōjo ni okeru Roshia shōbyōsha kyūgo no kentō" (Russo-Japanese War and Humanitarianism: Study of Relief Measures for Russian Invalids in the Matsuyama Asylum for POWs), 359 (617)-360 (618), http://www.law.nihon-u.ac.jp/publication/pdf/nihon/80_2/10.pdf, accessed July 1, 2017.

[87] Ibid. (both).

[88] Eliza Ruhamah Scidmore (1907).

[89] Ibid., 53.

[90] Ibid., 260.

[91] Ibid., 123-124.

[92] Ibid., 66, 181, 243.

[93] Ibid., 66, 243, 278-279; Lafcadio Hearn, *Kokoro: Hints and Echoes of Japanese Inner Life*, Boston, MA: Houghton Mifflin, 1896.

[94] Eliza Ruhamah Scidmore (1907), 89-90.

[95] Ibid., 269-272.

[96] Ibid., 56, 232, 263-264.

[97] Ibid., 293.

[98] Ibid., 359.

[99] Ibid., 355.

[100] "Matsuyama no kioku" (Memory of Matsuyama), April 28, 2009, http://seitousikan.blog130.fc2.com/blog-entry-373.html; Kita, 359 (671).

[101] "Matsuyama-shimin no Roshia-hei horyo ni taisuru 'o-mo-te-na-shi'" (Hospitality toward Russian POWs by Matsuyama Citizens), http://dayzi.com/a-izinkatuta2.html, accessed August 1,

2017; Eliza Ruhamah Scidmore (1907), 299-300.

[102] "Roshia-hei bochi" (Cemetery for Russian Soldiers), January 20, 2017, https://www.city.matsuyama.ehime.jp/kurashi/kurashi/bochi_nouk otsudo/russian_soldiers.html.

[103] "Hamadera horyo-shūyojō" (POW Internment Camp in Hamadera), *Sankei Shimbun*, July 27, 2013, http://www.sankei.com/west/news/130727/wst1307270065-n3.html.

[104] Eliza Ruhamah Scidmore (1907), 235-236; Maria Matsushima Junko, "Nagoya Seikyōkai to Roshia: Nichiro-sensō kara 21-seiki made" (Nagoya Russian Orthodox Church and Russia: From Russo-Japanese War to the 21st Century), *Oroshia-kai kaihō*, No. 17-3, February 3, 2011, http://www.for.aichi-pu.ac.jp/~kshiro/orosia17-3.html.

[105] Matsushima.

[106] "Shiberia yokuryū: Shin-shiryō 76-man nin-bun hakken" (Internment in Siberia: Newly Discovered Documents Had Data for as Many as 760,000 Detainees), *Tokyo Shimbun*, July 23, 2009; "The Geneva Conventions of 1949 and Their Additional

Protocols," https://www.icrc.org/eng/war-and-law/treaties-customary-law/geneva-conventions/overview-geneva-conventions.htm, accessed May 15, 2017. For details, see Mayumi Itoh, *The Making of China's Peace with Japan: What Xi Jinping Should Learn from Zhou Enlai*, New York: Palgrave McMillan, 2017.

[107] For a true account of Japanese prisoners of war in Siberia, see Mayumi Itoh, *"Hachi-ko" in Siberia: The True Story of Japanese Prisoners of War and a Dog*, Self-publication, distributed by Amazon, 2017.

[108] "Nichiro-sensō no, Nihonjin horyo."

[109] Eliza Ruhamah Scidmore (1907).

[110] Ibid., 344-345, 347-348.

[111] Ibid., 346-349.

[112] Ibid., 203-204, 278.

[113] Ibid., 9-13.

[114] George Kennan, *Tent Life in Siberia: Adventures Among the Koraks and Other Tribes in Kamchatka and Northern Asia*, New York: G.P. Putnam's Sons, 1870; George Kennan, *A Russian Comedy of Errors, With Other Stories and Sketches of Russian*

fe, New York: The Century, 1915.

[5] Eliza Ruhamah Scidmore (1907), 27-28.

[6] "Mikado Honors Americans: Order of the Crown Bestowed on urses and War Correspondents," *The New York Times*, July 4, 907; Eliza Ruhamah Scidmore (1907), 13.

[7] Eliza Ruhamah Scidmore (2002, trans. by Tonosaki), 472.

[8] Ibid., 472-476.

[19] Hasegawa Yūichi, "'Hainichi imin-hō' to Manshū · Burajiru" "Japanese Exclusion Act" and Manchuria · Brazil), in Miwa Kimidata, ed., *Nichibei kiki no kigen to Hainichi imin-hō* (Origin of U.S.-Japanese Crisis and the Japanese Exclusion Act), Tokyo: Ronsōsha, 1997, 44-79.

[120] "Webb–Haney Alien Land Act, California, 1913," http://www.intimeandplace.org/Japanese%20Internment/reading/c onstitution/alienlandlaw.html, accessed July 31, 2017.

[121] "The Immigration Act of 1924 (The Johnson–Reed Act)," https://history.state.gov/milestones/1921-1936/immigration-act, accessed July 31, 2017.

[122] "Hanami ga 100-bai tanoshimeri!..."; Eliza Ruhamah Scidmore (2002, trans. by Tonosaki), 473-475; "Miss Eliza Scidmore Dies in

Geneva at 72: Author of 'Jinrikisha Days in Japan' and Other

Books of the Far East." *The New York Times*, November 4, 1928.

123 Eliza Ruhamah Scidmore (2002, trans. by Tonosaki), 473-475;

Kusahara Katsuhide, *Nitobe Inazō, 1862–1933: Ware, Taiheihō*

no hashi to naran (Nitobe Inazō, 1862–1933: I Shall be a Bridge

over the Pacific Ocean), Tokyo: Fujiwara-shoten, 2012.

124 Kusahara; Samuel M. Snipes, "The Life of Japanese Quaker

Inazo Nitobe," August 1, 2011,

https://www.friendsjournal.org/life-japanese-quaker-inazo-nitobe-

1862-1933/.

125 Ibid. (both); Inazo Nitobe, *Bushido: The Soul of Japan*,

Philadelphia, PA: Leeds & Biddle, 1900. For details, see Oleg

Benesch, *Inventing the Way of the Samurai: Nationalism,*

Internationalism, and Bushido in Modern Japan, Oxford: Oxford

University Press, 2014.

126 Kusahara; Snipes.

127 Ibid. (both).

128 Eliza Ruhamah Scidmore (2002, trans. by Tonosaki), 471-476.

129 Ibid., 476; "Miss Eliza Scidmore Dies in Geneva at 72:…";

William Crozier, "Services in Memory of Eliza Ruhamah

hidmore, Held in Geneva, Switzerland, on Wednesday,

)vember 7, 1928, at the American Church," *Pamphlets in*

nerican History, 1988.

Eliza Ruhamah Scidmore (2002, trans. by Tonosaki), 476.

"Yokohama Foreign General Cemetery," http://www.yfgc-

pan.com/history_e.html, accessed May 31, 2017.

2 "History of the Cherry Trees"; "Hanami ga 100-bai

noshimeri!..."

3 "History of the Cherry Trees."

4 Ibid.

35 Ibid.; "The Story of Cherry Blossom Trees that Served …";

Mine no hana-oru shō-daitoku: Futatabi Shidomoa-joshi ni tsuite

Regarding Miss Scidmore Again: A Small Virtue of Cutting

Cherry Blossom Branches at the Mountain Peak). March 26, 2009,

https://madenokouji.wordpress.com/2009/03/26/.

[136] "History of the Cherry Trees"; "Neotani Usuzumi-sakura,"

http://www.city.motosu.lg.jp/sight/usuzumi/, accessed July 31,

2017.

[137] "History of the Cherry Trees."

[138] "Hanami ga 100-bai tanoshimeri!..."; Eliza Ruhamah Scidmore

(*Jinrikisha Days in Japan*), 29-30.

[139] "Hanami ga 100-bai tanoshimeri!..."

[140] "Eliza Ruhamah Scidmore: Jinrikisha Days in Japan," June 17

2017, https://blogs.yahoo.co.jp/mitch68canada/739333.html.